my broken pieces

my broken pieces

mending the wounds from sexual abuse
through faith, family, and love

....

ROSIE RIVERA

A CELEBRA BOOK

celebra

Published by New American Library,
an imprint of Penguin Random House LLC
375 Hudson Street, New York, New York 10014

This book is an original publication of New American Library.

First Printing, February 2016

LIBRARY OF CONGRESS CATALOGING-IN-PUBLICATION INFORMATION:

Rivera, Rosie, author.
My broken pieces: mending the wounds from sexual abuse through faith, family, and love/Rosie Rivera.
p.   cm.
ISBN 978-1-101-99006-3
1. Rivera, Rosie.   2. Women television personalities—United States—Biography.
3. Television personalities—United States—Biography.   4. Rivera, Rosie—Family.
5. Rivera, Jenni.   I. Title.
PN1992.4.R5313A3 2015
791.4502'8092—dc23   2015017328
[B]

Printed in the United States of America
10 9 8 7 6 5 4 3 2 1

Designed by Tiffany Estreicher

PUBLISHER'S NOTE
Penguin is committed to publishing works of quality and integrity. In that spirit, we are proud to offer this book to our readers; however the story, the experiences, and the words are the author's alone.

Penguin
Random
House

To Chay:
for planting the seed in my heart many years ago.
Sister, it now bears fruit.

To all the women who have suffered abuse:
you are not alone; we are sisters of brokenness.

To Jesus:
for becoming broken to make me whole.

Everyone is broken by life, but afterward
many are strong in the broken places.

—ERNEST HEMINGWAY

I first met Rosie Rivera at a *People en Español* event in Miami on October of 2012 where they were honoring powerful women in media. Her sister, Jenni, was chosen as one of them. Jenni actually nominated her sister to be part of the *poderosas* list too and the fans voted for her, so Rosie was chosen to give the keynote speech. I had never seen Rosie in person before, but as I sat watching her, the first thing that struck me was her beauty.

Then she began to tell her story. I recall that she was poised and eloquent as she recounted her sexual abuse as a child and the subsequent physical abuse she endured. My eyes welled up with tears, and my heart pounded as I heard about her years of pain and self-loathing, and the whole room of who's who in media was completely silent and mesmerized by her words. My teenage daughter was so moved that she told me she wanted to meet her. We went up to Rosie after the event, and I told her I wanted to interview her, not about juicy details pertaining to her sister, but about the Love Foundation and their work with battered women.

She was warm and welcoming to my daughter and myself, and we exchanged phone numbers. When we walked away, my daughter exclaimed, "Love her mom!" Teenagers are attracted to people who are real and raw, and Rosie was exactly that. As a journalist, I have been blessed to meet many people, and some I connect with more than others. I had immediate empathy for Rosie, and I realized that day that her story had the power to help and heal others.

Fast-forward three years, and as I read her book, *My Broken Pieces*, with so many uncensored details, once again, I am moved with compassion and sadness for Rosie and her family but also for so many young girls and boys who go through this pain but do not make it through to tell their story. However, for all the brokenness in Rosie's life, there is hope and beauty that outshines evil. This book is a powerful tool in healing especially for so many of us who are wounded souls. What I see through Rosie's life is that good does win in the end, and if God is on our side (and He never leaves us nor forsakes us), then we can find relief during the rough times, knowing that better days are ahead. Even in the midst of our darkest days, we can echo Rosie's belief that as it states in Romans 8:28: ". . . all things work together for good for those that love God," and I am just so grateful for that conviction too. Without it, so many of us would not be alive today.

My heart was uplifted as I read Rosie's story, and for all of you who have experienced loss, tragedy, abandonment, abuse and the darkest of days, remember that just as Rosie is alive and thriving today, so will you be. I pray that everyone who identifies with Rosie's story realizes that freedom from pain, guilt and hate is attainable. If there's one thread that is weaved throughout *My Broken Pieces*, it's that out of our brokenness, God can create a beautiful work of art.

introduction

Ever since I was a little girl, I knew I didn't want to go into show business. While I was growing up a Rivera, that was what everyone expected from me, but I had other plans. Whenever my dad would sit me on his lap in the morning and ask me what I wanted to be when I grew up, I'd say a teacher, a writer or an astronaut, but never did it cross my mind to become a performer. That was what my talented brothers and sister did, but not me. I was going to be just a great as them, but doing my own thing, whether traveling to the moon or writing a book.

But the summer I turned eight years old, everything changed. My dreams were all but destroyed. The sexual abuse I suffered and kept secret for so many years corroded my soul, and it wasn't long before I lost all sense of self-worth. The beautiful, wide world I had once dreamed of conquering suddenly collapsed and my universe turned dark. I started to believe, deep down in my heart, that I was truly worthless. The innocence of a golden childhood surrounded by so much love and affection faded to black.

For years, I woke up every morning hoping that the day ahead would be my last. All I could see around me was a world of suffering and endless pain, and no matter how hard I tried, I was unable to envision a life beyond the next day. I lived this way for eighteen years and could have continued that way for many more, had it not been for one simple discovery that changed my life.

The first time I told Chay that I wanted to write a book, she said, "Yes, Sister, go for it! You are going to be great! Your book will inspire so many people!" My big sister encouraged me from the very beginning, and while I knew this was what I had to do, the process wasn't easy. I had to relive and confront many difficult moments from my past. Yet in doing so, I discovered a very important lesson: that as long as you don't know your narrative, as long as you don't own your story, you will never be able to heal. Telling my story here has helped me understand parts of my life that I had never even thought about, and I truly hope that whatever hardships you are going through, these pages may help you understand that you are not a lost cause and you are not alone. God loves you and that is the biggest blessing of them all.

In order to tell my story, I had to first understand it, and if it hadn't been for God's guidance and steady hand, I would have never been brave enough to share it in these pages. But as vulnerable and exposed as I may feel by putting this out there, I know that there is a greater good, and today what matters most to me is to help others who have experienced sexual abuse. And God's love is there to remind you that you are beautiful and important to this the world.

It is my prayer that what you are about to read will give you the strength to know that whatever happens, there is hope. This book is not about simply being a survivor, but about living a richer, fuller and happier life.

That's why I want to say to you: If all you have is broken pieces, give them to God. He can mend them, heal them and utilize them for good. He wants the broken pieces you think everyone else has rejected. And no matter how lost or shattered you feel, I am here to tell you that life's pieces can be mended and restored.

contents

my broken pieces

looking for a way out

It was Saturday night and I was at my brother Lupe's house downing shot after shot of tequila. I'd been at it since the moment I
woke up that morning and like every other weekend I was feeling
pretty sorry for myself. I had just dropped out of law school, I was
being a lousy mother and I was failing at my job selling real estate,
and I was married to an abusive man. My brothers and sister were
traveling the world, taking it by storm while I was wasting my
life away smoking and drinking in seedy nightclubs, hoping that
the sun would never come up so I wouldn't have to face another
day. My family was the best anyone could ask for, but somehow
that wasn't enough—all I could think of was what an utter failure
I was and I couldn't see how things would ever get better. I was
stuck.

I took another shot of tequila and stared blankly at the wall.
This was a new low: I wasn't just sad and depressed. I was at a
point where I physically couldn't stand to be in the world anymore.
My head hurt from thinking so much and my body ached all the

time—I always felt as if I had just been beaten up. It wasn't just that I didn't want to live anymore. I couldn't. For as long as I could remember, I had been living with this death wish but that night something clicked inside me and I finally decided to take action. I decided I had to end my life once and for all. Nothing mattered to me anymore, not my loving parents, not my sister or my brothers. Not even my daughter Kassey, who was two at the time. Ever since she arrived in my life she had been a powerful reason to stay alive, but on this night not even the thought of her was enough to keep me afloat. I feared that all I could ever be to her was a disappointment and that she would probably be better off without me.

I could feel myself slipping so I dialed my brother Juan. Juan is the closest to me in age and if there is one person in the world who I know will always have my back, it's him. But when he picked up the phone, I could tell from the background noise that he was clearly in the middle of something.

"Sister, can I call you back in about an hour? I'm about to go onstage," he said.

"Yeah, sure," I said, trying to sound casual.

Of course he doesn't have time for me, I thought, wallowing in my self-pity. *Why would he?*

Next I tried to call my other brother Lupe, but he was probably onstage because his phone went straight to voice mail. So I finally decided to call my sister, Chay—no matter what I was going through, my big sister never judged me or made me feel like anything less than a warrior. She would get me out of this one. I needed so badly to see myself through her eyes, to believe that all the good things she thought of me were true.

"Hi, Sister, how are you?" I asked, doing my best to hide the tears in my voice. But it was impossible to keep a secret from Chay. Right away she knew something was up.

"Sister, don't cry," she said in her sweet voice. "I'm about to start my show but can I call you in about two hours? I promise I'll call you the minute I get offstage."

I hung up the phone thinking two hours were an eternity. There was no way I'd be able to hang on for so long. Every cell in my being was hurting and no amount of tequila or drugs was ever going to numb the pain. I needed it to stop.

It wasn't the first time I'd thought about killing myself. When I was sixteen and still dealing with the aftermath of what Trino had done to me, I tried to slit my wrists. But as soon as I saw the first flow of blood trickle down my arm I chickened out and pounced on the medicine cabinet, looking for a bandage. Part of it might be that when confronted with the reality of it, in my heart of hearts, I didn't want to die by my own hands. But more than that, I didn't want to offend God. Even though at the time I wasn't living a Christian life, I was terrified of going to Hell. No matter how much pain I was feeling right then, I knew committing suicide meant spending an eternity in Hell and that was something I wasn't willing to risk.

Nonetheless, over the following years death was always on my mind. At twenty-five, I was a single mother, my husband of three months was abusing me, and I felt like the loneliest person in the world. I walked around like an open wound, waiting for something or someone to give me the final blow. No matter how much my family tried to convince me of the contrary, in my eyes my life had no value. I wished for something to happen, something to put me in harm's way so my life would be finished. Every weekend I'd drink myself unconscious, do massive amounts of Ecstasy, and I'd sleep with random guys I'd pick up at bars while never once using protection. In my twisted mind, I went so far as hoping to get AIDS.

But nothing ever happened.

Now, drinking alone in my brother's house, I somehow wasn't afraid of Hell anymore. I believed that I was invisible to God. I knew He existed, was certain that He existed, but He was ignoring me. He clearly didn't care. Why else would He have allowed me to fall this low? This life already felt like Hell and so I figured the Hell that God was going to send me to couldn't possibly be any worse. I still didn't have it in me to take my own life, so the next best thing would be to find someone to do it for me. So I came up with a plan.

I was going to set off walking from Lupe's house in Playa del Rey toward South Central Los Angeles, a neighborhood notorious for being one of the most crime-ridden areas in the country. In my drunken mind, it all made perfect sense: in the time it would take for me to get there, there had to be at least one degenerate willing to pick me up, rape me, and kill me. Surely I couldn't be *that* lucky.

At around two thirty a.m., I started walking north on Lincoln Boulevard. I was wearing a tight black miniskirt and a revealing colorful top, which was bound to attract attention. But by the time I reached Loyola University—about half an hour into my journey—not a single soul had paid me one bit of attention. There were plenty of cars on the street but no one stopped to look at me twice. As much as I wanted to end my life then and there, there was also a part of me that was hoping someone would just stop and talk to me. But I was getting nothing. Clearly, I wasn't only invisible to God, I was also invisible to all of humankind. Was I really that unwanted? I had just lost eighty pounds, undergone a tummy tuck, and I looked better than I had in years. Why, then, was no one even noticing me?

I desperately needed to get someone's attention and if wandering down the street like a mad woman wasn't going to work, I needed to up my game. I took off half of the top I was wearing, and hiked my skirt up even higher. It was chilly outside and I could feel the cold wind from Marina del Rey engulfing me. I took off my high heels but my feet were too numb to feel any rocks on the cold concrete. If only my heart could have been as numb as my feet.

All I could hear was silence. Not a single car honked at me, not a single person stopped to ask me whether I needed help. There was just silence and the low hum of cars racing by. It was as if I was the only soul in the world and around me was absolute darkness, the confirmation of everything I was feeling in my heart. I remember looking up at the stars and screaming, "God! Why don't You just get rid of me? Why?" I yelled. "You allowed all the awful things in my life to happen so why don't You just let me go?"

I was only twenty-five, but felt as though I had lived a hundred years.

"Please, God," I begged, my face covered in tears, "if You care anything about me, I beg You, out of love, to take my life."

But yet again, nothing happened.

It had been a few hours since I'd had my last drink. My alcohol level had subsided enough that I was regaining some of my senses but not enough to deter me from my plan. My feet ached and I was starting to shiver, but I was desperate to find a way out. I continued to walk down the street, thinking of how to end my life.

The sun still hadn't come up by the time I finally decided to lie down in the street near the curb. I remember thinking: "I'll lie down here and fall asleep. Chances are, some drunk driver is bound to come barreling down this street; he won't see my body and will run me over without my having to feel a thing." More than dying, I was afraid of the pain and this would guarantee that it would be over fast.

"See, God?" I said to myself. "I don't need You. I can take care of this myself."

Exhausted, I laid my head down on the curb and fell into a deep slumber.

t w o

growing up rivera

Most people think the Rivera family is in the music business because of my father, Don Pedro Rivera, but the truth is my mother is the one who knows how to sing. My father has always loved music, but Doña Rosa, as everyone calls her—she's the real thing. She has the most amazing voice but unlike her husband and her children, she never wanted a career in music. She sings in the choir at church, but that's where her ambition stops. "I lost my children long before Janney's plane went down," she once said to me. "The bigger they get, the less I see of them." If she had it her way, we would all be living within walking distance of one another, surrounded by immediate family every single day. In fact, there was a time when we all did live within five minutes of her house on Ellis Street in North Long Beach. That was the happiest she has ever been.

Mom and Dad first met at a *concurso de canto*, a singing contest, when she was fourteen years old and he was fifteen. Mama was a good girl. She came from a family of eleven but when she was seven, she was sent away to live with her *madrina*, whom she was supposed to take care of in her *madrina*'s old age. From what Mother tells me, her godmother was not an easy lady to live with, and those years were no walk in the park. For the most part, she grew up devoid of any sort of affection and because she wasn't living at home with her own family, she never developed a relationship with her siblings, much less her parents. So when she met my father at the tender age of fourteen, immediately she fell in love. At the time, my father was selling lottery tickets on the street, an activity my grandfather—my mother's father—looked down on. My grandfather forbade my mother to see my father but for the first time in her life, she didn't care what he had to say. She loved Tata but passion for my father took over.

Not too long after they met, my mother and father packed their things and ran away together. My father took her in, married her, and cared for her from that moment on. He worked hard to provide the best he could, but those first years together were very difficult. They moved from *pueblito* to *pueblito,* living in itty-bitty shacks surrounded by lots of poverty, always looking for new opportunities yet not always finding them. Times were tough. To make things worse, at one point my mother's father managed to get my father thrown into jail for having run away with an underage girl. He served his sentence all while my mother patiently waited for him—she never complained about their situation and remained faithful to him. No amount of pressure or convincing was enough to make her change her mind. As soon as he got out, they went to live with my father's parents for some time until they got back on their feet.

While my father's family was more supportive, they were also very traditional, and I mean that in the worst possible sense. My paternal grandfather believed that a man should periodically hit his wife in order to make her submissive and obedient. My father didn't understand why he had to do it and, of course, neither did my mother. Yet she never complained to her children or family, never said anything bad about my father. She was *una mujer a la antigua*: no matter what happened, she always stood by his side.

My brothers Pete and Gus were born in Mexico and from the moment he became a father, Don Pedro Rivera became a devoted family man. He worked as many jobs as it took to provide for his family because for him, no matter what he's going through, no matter what he's doing, family always comes first. Always. And that's a value he engraved in all of his children's hearts. It's something we all live by.

With two little boys in tow, things only got harder. My parents did what they could to survive, but the situation wasn't getting any better, so in 1966 my father crossed the border to the United States, searching for work and better opportunities for his family. He went back and forth six times until finally, in 1968, he decided that it was time for my mother and the boys to join him. When they crossed the border to start a new life in Southern California, my poor mother was terrified. Not only was she moving to a new country and a new life, but also she was a few months pregnant with my sister, Jenni, or as I've always called her, Chay.

The first years in the U.S. were rough. Really rough. My father, a notorious self-starter, took several jobs—picking the fields, working at a plastic factory—all of which he hated. He is a self-made man and taking orders from others made him miserable. He continued with these jobs for a while until he was finally able to save up some money and decided to work for himself. He tried it all: he sold fruit at intersections, worked as a photographer at weddings, Sweet Sixteens, and *Quinceañeras*; he sold buttons at concerts, invested in beads for jewelry or curtains. . . . When we got our stands at the swap meet, we would sell anything and everything anyone was willing to pay for: fake nails, cassettes, and electronics. My father always said, if we have to sell diapers, we'll sell diapers! Anything was game. And through each and every one of his crazy ventures, my mom was right there by his side. At the swap meet, she manned one of the stands. When they started a bar, my mother was the waitress. When they started a restaurant, she was the cook. Any business he started, she was always one hundred percent with him, all while being a full-time mom to her children.

My father gets a lot of credit for what he's created and accomplished, but my mom was just as important in building the family business. She gave up everything for us to make it in this country. She has gone above and beyond for her family, and she even went as far as sacrificing her teeth. Around the early eighties, when Chay came up with the idea to make and sell buttons for the Menudo concert, my mom had been saving up for several years to get her teeth fixed. But my father's crazy business ventures always came first. So she gave him the money she had saved to buy the button machine. Sure enough, Chay made a killing selling buttons at the concert, and so my mother's teeth had to wait several more years as they built their new business.

Dad used that same machine to make buttons for the 1984 Los Angeles Olympics and with the fourteen thousand dollars in profits, he launched himself into yet another business venture: music production. One night at a bar, there was a mariachi band playing, and he really liked what he heard. After the show, the band members and my father got talking, and it turned out that they were looking for someone to help record their songs. My father, never one to shy away from a business opportunity, offered to do it himself.

They worked together to produce an album, which didn't end up being a bestseller, but that didn't deter my father. It was only a question of time before he'd find something that worked. He continued to look for talented banda, mariachi, and norteño artists and slowly began to create a small but loyal following within the Mexican-American community of Southern California. It's something no one had ever done before and there was clearly a hole in the market because business started to grow extremely well. In 1987, he launched his record label, Cintas Acuario, where he would eventually go on to discover and record such bestselling artists as Chalino Sánchez, El Chapo de Sinaloa, Graciela Beltrán, Rogelio Martínez, Paraíso Tropical de Durango, Lobito de Sinaloa, Canelos de Durango, Voces de Rancho and many many others, including my brothers and sister.

And because everything in the Rivera family is a team effort, as soon as Dad's business began to take off, it became the family business. We all worked, and any success was our shared success. Shortly thereafter, we opened Música del Pueblo, a record store on the Pacific Avenue retail strip in Huntington Park, yet on weekends you could still find our family selling cassettes at the Paramount Swap Meet.

As the youngest of six siblings, I grew up in adoration of my older brothers and sister. Gus and Pete had already left our parents' home by the time I was born, but Chay, Lupe, and Juan were still around and to me they were the coolest, funniest, kindest, smartest, most talented people in the world. When talking about the Rivera family, people sometimes say to me, "You're no one, you're just their little sister!" What they don't know is that's the biggest compliment anyone can give me. I love being their little sister! Being a part of this crazy, loving, talented, boisterous family is my greatest joy in life, the thing I am most thankful for.

My first memories of growing up are with Juan and Lupe. They are the closest to me in age since Juan is three years older and Lupe is nine years older. I admired Juan most in the world. He was the coolest guy I'd ever seen. He was super slick, and there was something about the way he acted, even the way he moved, that exuded so much confidence. He's always making people laugh and everyone is automatically drawn to him. At first, people tend to either love him or hate him, but once they get to know him, they love him all the same. When we were kids, you couldn't walk down the street without someone recognizing him. I thought he was a king. I followed him everywhere he went because I wanted so much to be like him.

To me, Juan has always been Juanelo or *Wualelo*, when I couldn't yet pronounce it correctly.

"*Wualelito, Wualelito,* wanna play?" I'd ask him.

At the time, Juanelo was obsessed with WrestleMania so I, too, became obsessed with WrestleMania. We would wrestle all the time. We'd usually play for a while, then inevitably something would happen and I'd go running to my mom to tell on him.

"*El Wuanelo me anda pegando!*" I'd say. "Juanelo is hitting me!"

And all my mother would say was "*Vas a ver, Juan, vas a ver . . .*" and I was so happy because it meant Juan was going to get it. I'd be so incredibly mad at him but then five minutes later, I'd forget what had happened and I'd be fine.

"*Wuanelito, Wuanelito,* wanna play?"

Juan is so forgiving that five minutes later he, too, would be okay. To this day, whenever we're on the phone and we start to get upset because we're not agreeing on something, I'll say to him, "Brother, I think we should hang up."

"Me too," he answers. "I'll talk to you later."

So we hang up and five minutes later one of us calls the other and says, "Wanna get something to eat?" And just like that, we're back to normal again, as if nothing ever happened.

In addition to wrestling, when we were little, Juan loved playing with cars and marbles, and since I wanted so badly to be like him, I became that girl. I never wore a skirt, never brushed my hair, hardly ever agreed to take a bath. I was the dirtiest little girl you'd ever seen but I didn't care! While other girls wore pretty dresses and played with dolls, all I cared about was playing outside with my brothers. The dirtier I was, the more fun we were having. It would drive my mother crazy. "Take off those dirty jeans! Get out of that big T-shirt! Brush your hair!" she'd yell. But before I could even say anything, my big brother Gus would step in.

"Mama, *deje a la güera que está hermosa* (Leave her alone, Mom, she looks beautiful)."

"See, Mom," I'd say with a gigantic smile on my face. *"¡Yo estoy hermosa!"*

As much as I loved spending time with my family, I absolutely detested going to the swap meet. And it's funny, when I read Chiquis's book, I was surprised to find out that she actually loved it! I couldn't stand it. I hated having to wake up early. I hated how dirty it was, how extreme the temperature changes were. In the morning, it was super cold and in the afternoon it was scorching hot and everything was filthy.

Back then, we didn't have allowances so whenever I'd ask my father for money, he'd simply give me a black trash bag and say:

"Here you go, *Hija*. Whatever you collect in cans . . . that will be your allowance."

It wasn't meant to be a punishment or anything; it was just the way it was. Because I saw my parents work so hard, every day, doing everything they could to make life better for us, I knew I had to pitch in. We all did. We were hard workers and you can say what you want about the Rivera family but one thing is certain: we have an unbelievably strong work ethic.

So my brothers and I would set out to find cans, picking through trash and crawling under cars. The cans were all full of trash and spit and loogies. I wanted to die. I was so grossed out, it was disgusting.

When I didn't set out on my can-gathering expeditions, I'd hang out with my mom at her stand at the swap meet and sometimes I'd fall asleep under one of the tables. My brothers Lupe and Juan would complain:

"Why does Rosie get to sleep while we're the ones working? Not fair!"

"Leave her alone," she'd say. *"Pobrecita mi niña.* My poor little girl."

But Lupe and Juan wouldn't give up and while I was sleeping they'd gather rubber bands and hit me with them. I'd wake up in pain and so angry! I became terrified of rubber bands as a result. For years, all they had to do was threaten to hit me with one to get me to agree to do something. In fact, to this day I am still scared of rubber bands.

My brother Lupe is the funniest, most outgoing, loving, business-savvy man you'll ever meet. He has always been like that, ever since he was a kid. He was so cute and extremely loving with me, the youngest woman in the family, but when it came to my mom he went all out with love. He was always kissing her and hugging her, always taking care of her. My mom used to say, "Lupe, you can't get married; you're going to leave me for your wife." Lupe is incredible at showing that he loves you. He goes overboard and when you're on the receiving end of all that love, it feels amazing.

When I was a little girl, he took care of me. One of the fondest memories I have of him is that whenever we were going somewhere—to school, the store, anywhere—he didn't want me to get lost so he'd make me hold his index finger. "Rosa," he'd say— he's the only one who calls me Rosa; I actually hate my name—"as long as you hold my finger you'll be okay." So whenever we were out on the street together, I would hold his finger tight. And he knew when I was scared because I would hold it even tighter. I'll never forget that feeling of being taken care of and being loved.

That isn't to say that Lupe wasn't a prankster like the rest of us. One day, Juan, Lupe, and I were home alone. When I was about six and Juan was nine, he would babysit me when my parents had to go out and do something and I just loved it. He would cook what he thought was an amazing meal: white rice and chocolate cake. I happened to love it so anytime Juan babysat me was a treat!

That particular day, Lupe was hanging out with us and after our sumptuous meal of white rice and chocolate cake, we were out in the garage playing and Lupe—who knew he could always count on Juan to do anything, no matter how stupid or crazy—suddenly pointed at a dark corner of the garage and said:

"Hey, Juan, you see that big old beehive over there?"

"Yeah, man, it's huge!" said Juan.

"Yeah, well, I think you should knock it down," said Lupe.

"Yeah?" said Juan, a glimmer of doubt in his eye.

"Yeah, I think you should get a big stick and knock it down," Lupe continued.

"All right!" said Juan, blindly following our big brother's lead.

So there goes Juan and right behind him was me, being nosy and never wanting to miss a thing.

First he tried hitting the beehive with a stick but when that didn't work, he grabbed some rocks. He started throwing them as hard as he could and suddenly the entire beehive came crashing down.

"Whoa, you did it!" I squealed with excitement. But as soon as I turned around, my brothers were nowhere to be seen. Juan had run back to the house as fast as he could. He flew through the door, while Lupe—who hadn't even stepped out into the garage—closed it right behind him. The bees were swarming all over the place and I was alone in the garage. I was terrified! I started banging on the door, begging them to let me in but the two of them just stood there laughing their heads off. They laughed and laughed and when I realized they weren't going to let me in, I had to run all the way around to the other side of the house in order to come in through the front door. I swear there was a trail of bees following me and once I got inside, my brothers were still laughing so hard they were out of breath.

"You guys are crazy!" I yelled. "You could have killed me! What if I'm allergic? I could have died!"

But Lupe just stood there very calmly and said, "No one told you to go outside, Rosa. I told Juan, not you."

That's how it always was in the Rivera household; we were always playing pranks on one another, making jokes, having the time of our lives. When we were older and saw the movie *Jackass*, it was like "Dude! My brothers did all that same stuff and for free!" Even my mom and my grandma had gotten so used to it that they would watch *Jackass* and sometimes comment among themselves: "*Ay, pues mira,* Juanito did that once . . ."

· · ·

The first house I ever lived in was on Gale Street in Long Beach. It was a small, bright green house right by the freeway but it had an enormous yard. *Surely we must be rich,* I thought, *to be able to afford such a huge yard!* My brothers and I spent day after day playing in that yard and we were never bored.

Even though the house was tiny, somehow we managed to share it with all sorts of animals—dogs, cats, rabbits, birds, and squirrels. One day, Dad even brought home a duck. The animals roamed freely around the house and we lived with them as if they were part of the family. Whenever an animal died, my brothers made up funny stories about it. That's why when Dad's duck mysteriously disappeared one day; my brothers told me it was because it had committed suicide. For some reason they thought that would make me feel better. (It didn't.)

We all learned to love animals, which is something that has been passed down from generation to generation. My kids, Chay's kids, Gus's kids, if they ever find an animal on the street, they bring it home and take care of it. I think I am the only one who kind of grew out of it. When I was about twelve or thirteen, one of our cats ate my two lovebirds. I absolutely adored those birds and it broke my heart! I felt betrayed and made a vow to never experience that again. I still respect animals, but I keep my distance and don't allow myself to get too attached.

For some reason, my older brother Pete, now Pastor Pete, went through a phase when he was about five years old, of being obsessed with killing animals. He would drown cats, grab them by the tail and toss them into a tree. He was probably just experimenting and understanding the meaning of life and death but it completely freaked my mother out, understandably. You'd hear her yell at the top of her lungs:

"Who killed another cat?" (At this point, it was "another" cat—that's how bad it was.) She would call Pete and Gus and ask them: "Who did it? *Díganme . . . quién?*"

And Pete and Gus would just stand there and act oblivious.

"I don't know! I don't know!" they'd whine.

"I know you know," she'd say, now fuming. "Which one of you was it?"

There would be a long pause, and then suddenly they'd both answer at the same time: "I did it! I did it!"

And Mom would never know, until years later, of course.

That's how it always went because growing up a Rivera, if there is one thing you know it's that you never, ever rat one another out. No matter what your brother does, no matter how bad it is, you never say a word. In fact, if one of your brothers is about to get caught, you throw yourself under the bus and take the blame. Pete and Gus must have been the first ones to start this unspoken rule that trickled down to the rest of us. Gus did it for Pete, Juan did it for Lupe, Chay, and me, I did it for Juan, and Chay, I'm sure, did it for all us. Because Chay and I were the girls of the house, we never got in so much trouble as the rest and in fact my brothers were under strict orders from my father never to touch us.

"No one can touch Janney, or Rosie," he would always say to them. "You can't hit them. *No one* can touch them."

Since as early as I can remember, Daddy filled me with positive affirmations. "You are strong. You are so smart," he always said to me. My father gave amazing encouragement to Chay and my brothers too. He wanted us to believe in ourselves, telling us that any dream could come true if we worked hard, were honorable, did things the right way, and didn't step on anyone to get to the top.

"Rosie, what do you want to be when you grow up?" he would ask me.

"Daddy, I want to be an astronaut!" I would exclaim.

"Well, *Hija*, then you can be the best astronaut in the world," he'd answer. I always believed him. I was surrounded by so much love and encouragement that I never once doubted that I could accomplish big and important things in the world. In my mind, all I had to do was work hard and all my dreams would come true.

My father never stopped asking me the same question over the years and every time I had a different answer. Later I would answer the same question with: "I want to be the first Mexican-American woman on the U.S. Supreme Court," or "I want to be a teacher."

And he replied, "Okay, but make sure you are the best teacher you can possibly be."

One day when I was about four years old, Mom was making a big breakfast for the family and I ran into the kitchen (as I did many mornings) and asked, "Daddy, Daddy! Can I sit on your lap while you eat?"

Dad never said no to me and that day was no exception. However, as soon as my mother put the big plate of scrambled eggs and tortillas in front of him, I suddenly felt a tickle in my nose and sneezed all over them.

There was a moment of silence before Mom rushed over and said to my father, "Don't worry, I'll cook you a new breakfast."

"No, you don't have to," he responded. "She's my daughter."

I felt so bad for having sneezed on his eggs but hearing him say that made me feel so special. With those simple words, he was telling me how much he loved me. He didn't have to say it—after all, I knew very well how much he loved me—but the fact that he did made me feel incredible. The next morning, when I got up, he was seated at the breakfast table and yet again I ran over to him with my arms outstretched, asking, "Papi, can I sit with you?"

Mom protested: "Don't let her, she might sneeze on your food again!"

But Dad didn't care. He picked me up and put me on his lap just like the previous morning. And sure enough, I sneezed!

Years later we found out that I was allergic to his cologne. Yet never once did my father withhold his love from me. Not even if it meant eating gross eggs!

Dad always said that Chay was his queen and I was his princess, and that was the way he treated us. There was nothing wrong with her being queen and me being a princess, it was just the way it was and I loved that we were the only two girls and that I was—and will always be—Chay's only sister.

Chay would say to me: "Sister, it's great that there is no other girl in our family because she would be the ugly one, she would be left out." And we'd laugh our heads off.

For as long as I can remember, my sister was my hero. Lupe and Juan were closer to me in age so they were my playmates, my everyday buddies, but my sister was the focus of my adoration. I followed her wherever she went, and even though she moved out of the house when I was about three years old, to me it never felt as though she didn't live with us because she was always over at our place. She always made time for me and when I was with her, I felt so special.

At the Gale house we shared a room, where Chay's Menudo posters were plastered all over the walls. She was in love with the Menudo boys and since I wanted to do everything she did, I thought I liked them too. So I'd jump on her bed to try to kiss them. One of those times, I jumped so high trying to reach the poster that I fell and hit my head hard.

When she saw the blood, my mother freaked out but my sister stayed super calm. She lovingly picked me up and never scolded me. Even though it was such a silly thing to do, jumping up and down to kiss a poster, she never once told me I was stupid or an idiot or anything. When she was upset with me, she would start her sentence with "Sister, I don't appreciate . . ." and then I knew I was in trouble. But she never made me feel bad about myself and that made me only love her more.

One day, she took me with her to Long Beach City College, where she was studying, and she explained what she did there. I must have been about six years old at the time and I thought, *Chay is the most amazing human being ever.* I wanted to be just like her, and right then and there I decided that no matter what, one day I was going to go to college.

I was Chay's baby. In fact Juan and I were her babies. Even though she had been praying for a baby sister, she fell in love with Juan the moment he came home from the hospital. And then when I came along, I became her *muñeca de carne*, her real-life doll.

When my sister would tell the story of my birth, she'd jokingly say that the day I came into the world, I changed everything. According to her, I ruined her twelfth birthday party. It was the biggest disappointment she ever had to confront, and she never forgot the terrible mark it left on her existence. Her birthday was on July second, and she was about to cut into her birthday cake when suddenly my mother's water broke, throwing everyone into a panic. My mother was rushed to the hospital, while all of my sister's guests packed up and left as quickly as possible. Several hours later I was born and Chay never recovered from such a scarring event. For years and years, my sister gave me the hardest time about this incident. Whenever she needed me to do something for her or when she just wanted to get her way, she'd say, "Sister, you owe me. Remember you ruined my twelfth birthday party? You owe me big time!"

And inevitably, I would cave in and do whatever it was she wanted me to do. It was her strongest bargaining chip, the one guarantee she could get her way.

Well, imagine my surprise when, years later, I found out through her book *Unbreakable* that the so-called birthday party, which I had spent years imagining to be this extravagant affair second only to Prince Charles and Diana's wedding, was just my sister and *two* girls! All this time I thought I had really ruined her birthday when it actually wasn't that big of a deal. I never had a chance to call her on it, but man, did she milk it. We will have an eternity to take it up with Jesus in Heaven.

Now if she genuinely did think I had ruined her birthday party, she sure got back at me four years later when her daughter Chiquis was born. Chay had just moved out of the house to be with her new husband, Trino, and Chiquis was her first baby. Although Chiquis was born on June twenty-sixth, the first time Chay brought her over to introduce her to the family was a week after the birth—also the day of my fourth birthday party. Chiquis was the most beautiful baby girl with big green eyes, and of course, Chay had to bring her to my party to steal the show. I was so annoyed! If you look at the pictures from that day, you can see that

I'm not looking at the camera or at the cake. I'm just staring directly at Chiquis, fuming with jealousy.

But then Chay said what she never stopped saying to me until her untimely death: "I love you, Sister. Don't worry. You'll always be my baby."

And she kept her promise because I always was.

three

love game

As I grew older, Mom finally came to her senses and understood
that no matter how hard I tried to make the best of it, I simply
hated going to the swap meet. And because I was the youngest and
I was able to get away with pretty much *anything*, she found ways
for me to stay behind. Sometimes she'd ship Juan and me off to the
recording studio with Dad. Tucked under the console, Juanelo and
I would spend hours playing with cars, Barbies, or anything we
had at our disposal. We'd listen to my father's artists do take after
take of the same song and from time to time my father would interrupt the recording to feed us a very balanced meal of Gatorade,
string cheese, and corn nuts. We loved it! Sometimes he'd feed us
that for three days straight but it never got old. Still today, any
time I eat corn nuts, I remember those long days hidden under the
console with my brother and I'm filled with a sense of nostalgia.
Back then, I didn't have a care in the world and everything about
my life was perfect.

Other times, when my father was also busy at the swap meet,

my mother would send me to my sister Chay's house. At the time, Chay was married to Trino, and Chiquis was about four years old. They were living in a mobile home in Carson, which to me was the best place on earth. I loved going there because not only did it mean I could spend the weekend playing with Chiquis; I would also get to spend time with my big sister. Their home was bright and quiet and even though it wasn't the most comfortable in the world, it sure beat hanging out at the swap meet.

Chay and Trino had gotten married in 1984 when she got pregnant with Chiquis. Their parents pressured them to get married and much to my brother's despair—he was heartbroken when Chay moved out and I was too young to really understand what was going on—Chay felt she had to leave our home and move in with the father of her child.

Chay met Trino when she was in eighth grade. She met him through a couple of her friends who took her to a chicken fast food restaurant where he worked and gave them a free meal. Soon enough Trino noticed my sister, my sister noticed Trino, and they fell madly in love. Who could blame them? Chay was, well, AWE-SOME and Trino was this charismatic and impossibly cool rocker dude; everyone in the neighborhood loved him and he seemed to have friends in all places. I distinctly remember seeing him at church on Sundays and noticing how loving and kind he was to everyone. He never raised his voice and later on when they had kids, he was always so gentle and patient with them. Chay's kids once told me that one night when they were driving back home after some event, they crossed the Long Beach bridge and seeing the big enormous moon over the water, one of the little ones said, "Look, Daddy, look how beautiful the moon looks!"

To which Trino responded, "You bet! And I'm gonna take you

to the moon tonight." It was such a sweet thing to say and it really showed how much he cared about the children. He always made them feel safe and cared for. Even I dreamed of going to the moon from that bridge.

Growing up, I loved Trino. Even though I always went over to be with my sister and my niece, Trino was always super kind to me, just as caring as he was with his own daughter Chiquis. He was like another big brother to me and I never once doubted that he was a great guy. Chay *loved* Trino and because I saw the world through my big sister's eyes, I couldn't help but love him too. My sister trusted him, so I trusted him too. Plus, he was impossibly cool and he said he loved my sister—what else could anyone ask for?

But as much as they loved each other, things between them were far from perfect. To say that Chay and Trino had a rocky relationship is putting it mildly. Even though for most of her life Chay was the woman we all remember today, this tough, fearless, powerful, strong woman who never let anything or anyone beat her down, back in those days, she could be quite submissive. I think she felt afraid and vulnerable—she wanted to make her marriage work—and I'll never forget the many times I heard Chay ask Trino not to leave her after one of their heated arguments.

In the summer of 1989—I was eight, and Chiquis was four—I spent a weekend at my sister's mobile home in Carson. Chay was pregnant with her second baby, Jacqie, and Chiquis and I were playing in her room without a worry in the world. Life couldn't get any better: I was hanging out with my sister and my niece, I didn't have to be at school and most important, I wasn't at the swap meet. It was a beautiful, sunny day and Chay was in the kitchen cooking my favorite food, of course, spaghetti and meatballs.

Chay would make these ridiculously *huge* meatballs and I loved them. Anytime I was over at her place, I'd ask her to make them for me.

But at some point when I walked into the kitchen, I noticed that there were no meatballs in what she was preparing. The meatballs being the best part, I said, "Hey, Sister, the spaghetti doesn't have any meatballs!"

"Oh! That's right," she said. "I wasn't going to make them this time."

"Oh, okay, Sister, no problem," I answered. I was disappointed, but within a couple of minutes I went back to playing with Chiquis.

Trino and Chay just started to live on their own without help from family, so they had very little money and their home had practically no furniture. In Chiquis's room, they had a dark blue rug and a worn-out green-and-blue San Marcos blanket—every Mexican family has one—spread down on the floor for her to play on. Warm rays of sunshine streamed through the open windows and the room felt bright and airy. It was one of those beautiful, picture-perfect days when the colors are so bright, you feel as if you're in a movie. Chiquis and I were sitting on the blanket playing with Barbie dolls; our game was so beautiful and innocent, two little girls dreaming up a fantasy world of queens and princesses and balls. Suddenly we heard Chay and Trino start fighting. Trino and Chay were always fighting, so we were unfazed by the screaming and just continued on with our game. But a few minutes later we were surprised to hear a door slam. Startled, Chiquis and I ran into the living room to see who had left. We found Trino standing alone in the kitchen.

"Where's my sister?" I asked him.

"She went to get you some meatballs," he answered. "She'll be back in a bit, don't worry."

"Oh, okay," I said and returned to my game with Chiquis. It was strange for my sister to leave without saying good-bye but I figured it must have meant that she was in a hurry or something. I was just happy she was going to make the meatballs after all.

Chiquis and I went back to playing with the Barbies. A few minutes later, Trino popped into the bedroom.

"Chiquis, go play outside," he said sternly.

"Why?" asked Chiquis. "I don't want to!"

"I'm telling you, go play in the living room! Go watch TV or something!" he said, this time in a harsher tone.

It was so rare for him to yell at Chiquis that she immediately understood there would be no more negotiating. She immediately left and Trino closed the door behind her. Although it did seem strange to me that he would yell at Chiquis, I didn't necessarily think anything was wrong.

"Do you wanna play a game, Rosie?" he asked.

"Sure!" I answered. "What kind of game?"

"It's the love game," he answered.

"Cool!" I said. I didn't understand why Chiquis couldn't play with us but decided just to go with it.

Trino asked me to put my Barbies aside, close my eyes, and lie down. I froze as he pulled down my shorts, leaving me in my underwear and the short blue top I was wearing that day. He covered me with the San Marcos blanket and then slowly began to kiss my neck. I could feel his warm breath on my skin and the wetness of his kisses felt strange. Still, I didn't understand what was going on but I trusted him and wasn't really afraid since I was doing as told. Trino had said it was a game and as long as we were playing, I knew I would be all right.

But Trino continued to kiss and touch me. He slid his large hand between my thighs and slowly made his way up into my underwear. Confusion took over and I felt uncomfortable. Although something definitely felt wrong, I didn't exactly understand what I was feeling. Trino's fingers felt coarse against my skin as he gradually touched me in places I had never been touched.

Suddenly the door flung open. It was Chiquis. I'll never forget the look on her face when she saw us.

"Oh, are you going to do to her what you do to Mommy?" she asked.

"Get out!" Trino immediately yelled back at her and Chiquis scurried away.

That's when I freaked out. That's when I knew something was definitely wrong. What kind of game was it that Chiquis couldn't play? And why in the world would he play it with me if he played it with my sister? Would Chay be upset that I was playing it too?

I didn't know what to think. I didn't want to do anything to upset Chay yet I didn't want to upset Trino either. I was surprised and confused and frozen into silence.

Moments later, Trino simply got up and left. He didn't say a word or even look at me. He just left. While what he did to me that day didn't physically hurt, the feeling that ultimately stayed with me was that he left me there, all alone. One moment he was all over me, giving me attention and telling me he wanted to play with me, and the next he was discarding me like a piece of trash, leaving me alone, vulnerable and half-naked. I felt ashamed and my mind simply couldn't process what had just happened.

I don't remember the rest of that day. Most of my recollections come to me in flashes: the San Marcos blanket, the blond Barbie dolls, the bright blue sky, the look on Chiquis's face. I know that eventually Chay came home and we all sat around the table and ate the spaghetti—and giant meatballs. For many years after that, once I fully understood what happened that day, I couldn't bring myself to eat spaghetti and meatballs. The mere thought of it made my stomach turn.

That day was the beginning of a nightmare that would last several years, and the blurry memories of what transpired often came back to me. I'd obsess and think of all the ways in which I could have avoided it, what I could have done to stop it from happening. *If I hadn't asked for meatballs, Chay wouldn't have left . . . If I hadn't said yes to his stupid game and just kept playing with Chiquis . . . If only I'd gone to the swap meet with the rest of my family . . . God . . . How stupid could I be?* Time and time again, I blamed myself for everything that happened that day and from that day on, I thought I even deserved it for being so stupid. It took me many years to understand that it wasn't my fault: I was just a little girl at the time and there was nothing I could have done to stop him.

That same summer, on another beautiful sunny day, I found myself alone in the bathroom with Trino. I'm not sure how I got there or why, but I do remember the exact moment with a certain degree of clarity.

Trino was sitting on the toilet and we were, once again, playing the "love game." He pulled down his pants and I saw he was erect. I had never seen a naked man before, let alone an erect penis, so I had no idea what it meant. I was so worried that he'd get upset and leave me again that I tried my best to stay calm. In a strange way, even though I suspected that what we were doing was wrong, I still wanted Trino to be pleased with me. I didn't want him to walk out and leave me the way he had the previous time. So even though this time I was a little more aware of what the "love game" entailed, I didn't offer any resistance.

Trino sat me on top of him and I felt something hard between my legs and then right away I felt excruciating pain. It felt as if he had put a knife inside me. The pain was so sharp and so intense that I was convinced he had a knife and that he was cutting me.

"OUCH!" I screamed from the top of my lungs. "It HURTS!"

There must have been someone outside because as soon as I let out that scream he quickly covered my mouth with his hand— letting me know, in no uncertain terms, that I had to keep my mouth shut.

"If you say one word about this, I will kill your brothers, and your sister," he whispered loudly into my ear. "Do you hear me?"

That's when I understood something was really not right. I was hurting, I was in pain, and not only was he not concerned; he didn't want me to tell anyone. That's when I understood that this "game" wasn't a game after all nor was it for children.

A thousand thoughts raced through my mind as I tried to make sense of what was going on. *Was Chay going to die? Was he going to hurt her? And my brothers?* I was scared and in so much pain but ironically what worried me the most was that Trino was upset. He was visibly annoyed (probably because he hadn't been able to fully penetrate me) and I didn't know what to do because I never annoyed anyone! I was the baby in this big loving family and all in all, I was a great kid; no one ever had any reason to be annoyed at me. All I wanted was for him to stop being upset at me—I didn't want him to hurt me but most important, I didn't want him to hurt Chay. I looked up at him and without even meeting my gaze, he simply tossed me to the side, got up, and left. At that point, the pain was so excruciating that I thought I was bleeding, and in my eight-year-old mind that surely meant death. *Why is he leaving me here?* I thought. *How can he abandon me when I'm in pain and I need him? Is Chay really going to die?* From then on, I begged my sister not to die. I would tell her that without her I would go crazy, get depressed and die too. My sister didn't know why, but my greatest fear was to lose her.

I could barely make sense of these many thoughts swirling in my head. The pain between my legs eventually subsided and I later checked to find that there was no bleeding. But that feeling of abandonment—and the fear of losing Chay—never left me for many years to come.

Just as I don't remember much else about that day, my memory of the rest of that beautiful summer is equally blurry. The time spent with Chay and Chiquis, moments at home with my brothers and parents. Everything that wasn't the abuse just disappeared from my mind. Gone.

There are so many horrible things about abuse and I've had many years to reflect upon the ways in which Trino's actions affected the rest of my life. But one of the things that hurt me the most was losing my childhood memories. I remember very little between the ages of eight and eleven and no matter how much therapy I have or how hard I try to remember, that's something I will never get back.

The thing is, in so many ways I live off my childhood memories. I love remembering my family, laughing at all our crazy stories, reliving the great times we shared together. My family is my rock, my foundation. They are what I live by and whenever times are difficult, whether it's a family issue or my own personal problems, those memories are what fuel me. At the time I was being abused or even later, when my life seemed so grim that I could barely hold it together, the love of my family kept me afloat. Knowing that there are precious memories lost to me forever tears me up inside. I tried so hard to block out the bad stuff that I also lost all the good stuff along the way. When I think back to that afternoon when my sister was making spaghetti and meatballs for me, it kills me to think that Chay made my favorite meal and I can't even remember eating it.

If ever I had felt love for Trino for being my sister's husband, it all disappeared the instant I understood that there was something very wrong with his game. Things got strange whenever I was alone with him so I decided that the best way to deal with the situation was making sure I was never alone with him again. *Just stay away from him,* I thought. And that's what I did. Despite how much I hated it, I started to go to the swap meet again. But my sister missed me and it was so hard for me to be away from her that I'd still end up going to their place from time to time. But whenever I was there, I made sure I stuck close to my sister and shadowed her every move.

As time went by and the reality of what Trino did to me kicked in, I started to ask myself so many troubling questions: *Am I the only little girl this happens to? Or do men do this all the time and nobody talks about it?* I would watch TV for hours and hours, trying to escape my reality but also just wishing someone would come out and talk about what I was going through. *Surely, this must happen to other girls,* I thought. But no one did and I was left feeling lonelier than ever.

I started to become more and more of an introvert. I hated Trino with all my being but the truth was I hated myself even more. I feared him for what he was capable of doing to me but deep in my heart what was destroying me was that I despised myself for allowing the abuse to happen. I compared myself to all the strong personalities in my family and I saw myself as weak, no more than a coward.

I ceased to be the cheerful child I had been prior to the abuse, and I began to pull back from my family in so many ways. I'm sure they all noticed but no one ever confronted me about it. I guess in their eyes I was just being rebellious.

Soon I found myself starting to lose trust in all men, thinking every one of them could be like Trino, even my brothers and father. I never tried to discuss this with anyone so the thoughts just grew in my head and before long I went from wondering whether all men were the same to believing it with absolute certainty. Juan had always been my hero and I would do whatever he asked of me. But when this started happening with Trino, I suddenly stopped wrestling with him. While I used to throw myself on the ground with him, tossing, tumbling, and tickling each other until we turned blue in the face from laughing so much, I wouldn't even let him near me. The little sister who had cuddled, loved, and followed him all around the place now drew away, and he didn't understand why.

"Don't touch me!" I'd yell at him. "Don't hug me! Back off!"

"What's wrong with you?" he'd ask, bewildered.

"You're gross! Get away from me!"

And Juan wasn't the only one who'd lost me, so had my father. I no longer wanted to jump on his lap for breakfast and whenever he tried to hug me or kiss me as any father would want to hug and kiss his child—his little princess—I would shrug away. It broke my father's heart to see me behave that way, but he was always respectful of my wishes, so he left me alone.

The only thing I remember caring about in those days was reading. I'd spend hours escaping into my favorite books— somehow it was comforting to read about realities that were so far removed from my own. In my mind, I had rehearsed a thousand times what I would do if Trino ever approached me again, and I decided that I would just shut down and let my mind wander to faraway places. I must have read every single book in *The Baby-Sitters Club* series so whenever Trino did manage to get close to me, I would shut my body down and escape into my dreamworld, thinking about my favorite characters. While he touched me, I would close my eyes and imagine I was Claudia. Claudia lived in New York and she was really into fashion so I would create a whole fantasy in my mind where I was just like her. I lived in my own apartment in New York and was into fashion, beautiful and popular. Focusing on these stories allowed me to escape from the reality of what was happening to me and it allowed me to hold on to the little bit of self-love I had left.

I don't remember anything else about being ten. All I knew was that I had to focus on staying away from Trino. My poor sister had no idea what was going on, nor did anyone else. I was so afraid that he would kill my sister that I took extra care not to let anyone else find out. If I happened to find myself in the same room with Trino, I would quickly slip out before anyone noticed. I thought I was being subtle but soon enough Trino realized what was going on and he asked:

"Why do you stay away from me?"

Isn't it obvious? I thought, but I wouldn't say anything and just run away to play.

By the time I was about eleven years old, Chay and Trino had moved into a house on Fifty-fifth Street in North Long Beach, on the block behind my mother's house on Ellis Street.

One afternoon I was over at their place, visiting my sister. Trino was outside doing something on the car and I was sitting on the porch. It was a quiet, peaceful afternoon and I was making sure I stayed away from Trino, barely speaking to him unless it was absolutely necessary. I was always afraid of him but somehow being out in the open like that, I didn't feel so threatened. Suddenly, in the most matter-of-fact way, Trino said to me:

"Hey, Rosie, do you want to learn how to drive?"

And immediately forgetting everything, I jumped up and yelled: "Yeah!"

My brothers learned to drive when they were twelve and my brothers were the coolest people in the world to me. Of course I wanted to learn how to drive! Of course I wanted to be like them! I didn't even stop to think twice about what might happen if I was all alone in a car with Trino. All I wanted was to learn how to drive. I was still this innocent little kid. Thinking back, I'm infuriated that I let my guard down so easily. I spent many years asking myself, how could I have been so stupid? How could I have been so naive? How could I have forgotten it all at the mere mention of learning how to drive?

"Okay," said Trino as he pulled himself up from under the car. "But you're going to have to sit on my lap."

Trino climbed into the driver's seat and motioned for me to get in.

"Okay!" I answered, *ahí va la mensa,* and I climbed onto his lap.

"I'll do the feet because you can't do them and you can do the wheel," he explained.

Trino revved up the engine and there I was sitting on his lap, so happy I was driving that I forgot all fear, all confusion . . . everything that had happened. For that instant, I was just a happy little girl learning how to drive.

We hadn't gotten to the end of the block when I started to feel his hand under my skirt, trying to get into my panties. And I immediately remembered: *Oh my God, I'm alone with him, we're in a car, my sister isn't near. This is not good.*

I was so scared that I just started begging him: "Please don't. Please don't do this to me. Please."

Trino got upset and after a while of listening to me beg he tossed me over to the passenger seat. That time, he didn't do anything to me but I remember thinking I was an imbecile. How could I have possibly forgotten?

I never wanted to fall in his trap again and because I couldn't trust myself completely, I promised myself something that day: No matter what Trino—or anyone—ever offered me, I would always say no. I would systematically always say no.

four

dark times

Sexual abuse changes everything you've ever been told. My father had always told me I was a princess and I could conquer the world and be whatever I wanted to be. But once the abuse started, my bubble burst and everything I had ever believed about myself came crashing to pieces. I realized I was no princess—how could a princess be a part of something so dirty? How was I ever going to conquer the world? I wasn't even able to get away from Trino! Slowly, I started to believe every single twisted thing my mind told me and I completely forgot all of my dad's lessons and positive af-firmations. The only thing I knew for sure was that family was most important. Everything other than that became a lie. I was worthless. I was dirty. I was weak. I didn't deserve anything good because deep down in my mind, I believed I wasn't good. I *knew* I was a bad person.

I stopped speaking. I became a difficult, gloomy child who wouldn't let anyone near her. At the time, I had a diary and while now I think writing could have been a way to reflect and release during such a difficult time, I stopped altogether. I was too afraid that someone might read it and then my life would really be over. Trino never repeated the threat of killing Chay if anyone ever found out about our little secret, but in my mind, it was on repeat every time I saw him. I was genuinely terrified of losing my sister, so the thought of saying anything was out of the question. Chay's life became my responsibility and if it meant that I had to endure all the pain and humiliation on my own, then that's what I was going to do.

Keeping the secret of sexual abuse forces you to live in a continuous lie. You lie to the people around you and you also lie to yourself. Your entire belief system is turned upside down and you start to question everything you've ever known to be true, including the concepts of love, desire, and affection. Trino had said that the game we were playing was called the "love game," but I didn't know what that really meant. *Are love and sex the same thing? Is sex what people do to show they love each other? What about my parents and my brothers—they don't do this to me. Does that mean they don't love me? Is Trino the only one who loves me? And if he loves me, then why does he hurt me?*

Over the course of that summer, everything—absolutely everything—in my life changed. I could no longer stand my brothers, whom I had always adored; I was afraid of my loving father; I was terrified that my sister might die. Life became a series of extremes, and there was nothing in between to make me feel stable. Everyday life continued its pace while my soul became a black hole that was sucking the life right out of me. Even the things I used to enjoy, like playing with my Barbie dolls, became tainted with my experience of sexual abuse. My Barbies were my only witnesses that day in the mobile home and although I hardly played with them anymore, when I did, the dolls would inevitably end up having sex with each other.

Everything around me became sexualized, and I no longer knew the difference between what was normal and what wasn't. When your body is exposed to sex at such a young age, you don't yet have the maturity to understand what you are feeling. Your body just wakes up. The sexual desire that grows inside you doesn't know how old you are or who is touching you; it doesn't know that it's your brother-in-law or that it's incest. It just knows that it feels good. So you start craving sex and looking for it in everything around you.

I understand this now that I have read the books, done all the work, and gone to therapy, but at the time my mind couldn't process why I was craving something I hated so much. I hated my body because my body liked what my heart and my mind clearly didn't. *What's wrong with me?* I asked myself over and over again. *Sex is gross!* But no matter how much I tried, I couldn't stop myself from feeling what I was feeling.

By the time I was eleven, I became addicted to porn. I would look for it on TV or find magazines, looking at anything I could get my hands on. I'd hide in my room to watch as quickly as I could and then when everything was done, I'd rush to hide or throw everything away, feeling so dirty and ashamed. I'd promise myself that I was never going to do it again, but the next day I would start all over again. It became a vicious cycle that haunted me for many years to come.

At school I had to take a sex ed class as part of the fifth-grade curriculum. In order to introduce us to the facts and realities of sex, our teachers showed us illustrations of the male and female anatomy, and we talked about reproductive cycles, contraception, unplanned pregnancies, STDs, and so forth. When the teacher showed us a picture of a man's unerect penis, the other girls started giggling and acting very nervous. Why were they being so silly? I wondered. Hadn't they seen naked men before?

I couldn't understand what they thought was so funny. I thought to myself, *That drawing is wrong. It doesn't look like that,* because, of course, I had seen it differently. As I glanced around the classroom, it suddenly hit me: wait a minute, I'm the only one who isn't giggling!

I was livid. I realized that no matter how hard I tried, no matter what I did or said, I was never going to be a normal girl like most. By sticking his penis inside me, Trino had made me abnormal and nothing would ever go back to being the way it was. Trino robbed me of my innocence, my memories—he robbed me of my childhood.

As the classroom laughter swelled up around me, I felt nauseated. I asked the teacher for permission to go to the bathroom, where I threw up.

Every summer, my family would go down to Mexico for vacation. For our parents, it was always very important that we know Mexican culture. Even though most of us were born in the United States, we all grew up speaking Spanish at home and feeling very proud of our Mexican heritage. In fact, for the longest time I felt upset that I wasn't *really* Mexican or even Mexican enough.

I loved our yearly trips to Mexico and during the years in which Trino was abusing me, those trips brought me a great deal comfort. They were a brief break from the darkness that had taken over my soul. Hundreds of miles away from my everyday life, it was almost as though I was allowed to be a little girl again: my brothers and I would spend long summer days playing outdoors with our cousins and the neighborhood kids, running around and having all the fun we had at home, just surrounded by even more kids and family members. Juan and I would use the huge rock behind my grandma's house at El Cerro de la Campana as a slide. We would feed Nana Lola's chickens and play basketball until midnight at the park. We'd play video games and watch TV, just like back home, but I loved playing in the street and knowing I was safe.

We usually stayed at my maternal grandmother's house but I spent most of my time playing with my cousins, Juana and María. They were slightly older than me, they were *real* Mexicans, and to me they were impossibly cool so I followed them around like a shadow. Back home, I got to play games only with my brothers, so playing with girls was refreshing and new—a welcome change, especially at a time when I couldn't stand to be near the opposite sex. Being around them felt comfortable and easy and I didn't have to be constantly on the lookout for what might happen. I felt safe.

That's why when one day, Juana suggested that we play *a la mamá y el papá*, I thought nothing of it. One of us was supposed to be the dad, another one of us was supposed to be the mom, and she instructed us on how to "make a baby." María and I would follow her instructions and with clothes on, we lay on top of each other while we fake-kissed on the mouth and on the neck, slowly rubbing our bodies together in fake sexual movements. The whole thing wouldn't last more than a minute, and after that, pouf! We had a baby and we continued with our game.

Even though our movements were pretty graphic and somewhat reminiscent, in my mind, of what happened with Trino, I didn't know I was doing anything wrong. After all they were girls and because they never hurt me I trusted them and knew that it was just a game. We—all three of us—were playing together so I was never in a position of weakness. It was more like an exploration of a topic. I was so confused by my sexuality that I was seeking anything that would help me decipher what I was going through.

Everything I did with Juana and María felt so normal and nonthreatening that when I got back home from Mexico that summer, I innocently suggested to one of my girlfriends that we play *al papá y a la mamá* and I taught her what Juana had taught me. Whenever she came over to my house, we played the same game over and over again without me ever realizing what I was doing. In my mind, I was simply replicating what my cousins taught me. Now I realize that my actions had much more serious consequences than I could have ever imagined but at the time it came from a completely innocent place. I never wanted to hurt this girl and to this day, even though we have talked about it at length and she understands the circumstances of what led me to act that way, I feel guilty for what I did and I hope that one day she will forgive me.

It would be easy for me to look back and blame Trino or Juana or María for what I did, but when it comes to my actions, I know that there is no one else to blame but myself. Yes, Trino abused me; yes, that destroyed my sense of normalcy and clouded my ability to tell right from wrong, but there is a point where my decisions are my own and I have to take responsibility for what I have done.

Thinking back on this and having read a lot on the topic of sexual abuse, I wonder if Juana and María were two little girls who, like me, knew way too much about sex for their age. Who knows . . . maybe, like me, they were abused at some point and, in the same way Juana and María were innocently replicating what someone did to them, I was replicating what they did to me with someone else. We were children playing grown-up games without even understanding what it meant.

For years I have tried to keep up with Juana and María and I pray to God that if they have been through anything similar to what I've been through, they may find peace.

"Time is your best friend," is what people say when you are trying to get over something and while it can be true for when you are getting over a breakup, it's not the case for sexual abuse. Not only did the abuse affect the way I acted; it all but destroyed my self-esteem and hopes and dreams. As time went by, I became more and more chained to the lies I had constructed in my brain. My sadness grew, my anger grew, and with each passing day, I hated myself more. Just a few years earlier, I had wanted to become an astronaut, a writer; I had wanted to travel the world, learn about art. One by one, I buried each and every one of those dreams, and all I really wanted was to die. In my heart of hearts, I knew God was out there somewhere, but I never really tried to reach out to Him. I didn't understand why He had allowed this to happen to me. Here was my thinking: if I could not trust the father I could see, and didn't believe he would protect me, how on earth could I be sure that the God I couldn't see cared about me? In my mind, I came to the conclusion that He didn't notice me or love me enough to keep me safe. Alone and depressed, I didn't know who I could turn to. The only person I knew who loved me unconditionally was my sister, Chay, but I couldn't bear the thought of telling her the truth.

For countless days and countless nights, I prayed for *something* to happen that would make my life better.

Life didn't get any better but something did happen: at the age of eleven my body started to change and I got my first period. Then, as if magically, Trino stopped abusing me. He told me that he didn't like girls with pubic hair so the abuse stopped. Just like that. It was a huge relief, of course, but the invisible wounds left behind after those three awful years are something I continue to deal with to this day.

As adolescence started to kick in, I became more and more unhappy. I gained a lot of weight and felt terrible about my body and myself. I'd look at my sister and my mother, wanting so bad to be as strong and powerful and loving as they were but I knew in my heart that I would never be like them because I had a secret—a dirty secret that made me unworthy of the life I was given.

About a year after the abuse stopped, Trino and Chay's rocky relationship finally imploded. They separated and my mom would often babysit Chay's three kids—Chiquis, Jacqie, and Michael—while Chay worked two jobs. I knew my sister was going through a particularly rough patch but at the same time I was deeply grateful that I wouldn't have to be around Trino anymore. Even though all signs indicated that he was never going to abuse me again, as long as he was in our lives I continued to live in fear. I was afraid of being near him and given his threats on her life, I sure didn't want my sister to be near him either.

Trino continued to have a relationship with the kids and on weekends he would come by our house to pick them up. I remember one Saturday, when I was twelve, I was home alone when he came knocking at the door, looking for the kids. A sharp pang of fear shot through my body—the last thing in the world I wanted to do was to let him in.

He knocked and knocked, yelling, "Open the door. I want to see my kids! Let me in!"

"They aren't here," I answered through the door. "I promise! I don't know where they are." I tried to sound as casual as possible but I was terrified.

Trino kept banging and banging so, knowing there was a screen door between us and I was somewhat protected, I opened the front door.

As soon as he saw me, he said: "Don't worry, I'm not going to do anything to you. You're much too fat!"

I wanted to die. After everything Trino had done to me, to hear him call me fat made me feel even worse than I already did. In a twisted way, for all those years, Trino had been my measure of self-worth and part of me had wanted to believe that he did what he did to me because he actually loved me. Of course he didn't love me but his words were the confirmation of everything I dreaded most: I was fat, ugly, and unworthy of love.

I plunged deeper into my depression and by the time I turned thirteen, I weighed one hundred seventy-five pounds. I would cry every night because it was difficult, especially at my age and in our family, to be overweight. My father and brothers and sister were the entertainers, but Dad said I represented the family whether I sang or not. He was sure I'd end up in entertainment no matter how much I refused, and in his eyes everyone was supposed to stay in shape, look their best, and smile at the cameras.

Despite living with the pain and anguish over my obesity and what Trino put me through, I figured that if Trino didn't want me because I was fat, then other men wouldn't want me either. And that was okay with me. I would rather take the pain and humiliation of the weight gain any day over the torture of sexual abuse.

That same year, I found out that Chiquis was going through some difficulties of her own. I had always seen Chiquis as my adorable little niece, my first friend, my sister's princess. To me, she was the luckiest little girl in the world because she was my sister's daughter and I thought nothing could ever go wrong for her.

Yet while she had the best mother in the world, Trino—the man who had tormented me for the past five years—was her father. I had grown to hate Trino with every fiber of my being, but I never thought he was anything less than a great father to his kids. Chiquis adored him and I remember that even after he abused me, he would come to church and sit in the front row with Chay and the kids. He'd sing the songs and smile, always greeting everyone so warmly. Although I knew the truth about him (and so did God), when I saw him at church like that, it always made me wonder whether it was all a figment of my imagination. How on earth could anyone be so duplicitous?

But the nature of his true self was again confirmed during the summer before I went to high school. Chiquis was ten years old at the time. I was on the phone with a friend.

"*Tía*, can we talk?" she said.

"Of course, baby. What's up?" I answered.

"I know why you hate my dad so much," she said.

I didn't quite understand where she was coming from, but her statement immediately made me feel exposed. Could it be that after so many years she remembered what had happened in the mobile home?

"Oh, yeah?" I answered somewhat on the defensive. "Why?"

"I know because what he did to you he does to me."

I'll never forget those words. My heart simultaneously sank and exploded in rage. I wanted to kill Trino, right then and there, but at the same time I also felt incredibly guilty—how was it that I had been so wrapped up in my own drama that I didn't see what he had been doing to my sweet Chiquis?

We danced around the subject, but it took only a few minutes for me to understand exactly what was going on. Trino was abusing Chiquis whenever the kids stayed with him over the weekend. I was appalled. I couldn't believe what she was telling me. I thought there was something wrong with me, and that was why I'd been abused. But how could he be doing such a horrible thing to his precious little daughter? How could he be hurting Chiquis?

My mind was spinning. I didn't know what to do. If I couldn't defend myself against his abuse, how in the world was I going to defend Chiquis? Who was I going to tell? What was I going to do? The questions kept piling up and yet no clear answers emerged.

Chiquis and I were both extremely uncomfortable so we didn't discuss too many details, but from what she told me, it sounded as if Trino hadn't touched her in a while so we both hoped that meant it was over. Instead, we decided to pray for him because it was clear he was sick or emotionally damaged. Chiquis was just as afraid of telling her mom as I was, so we made the promise never to say a word. I made her promise to tell me if he did it again and we would confess to our family. Maybe that's why she stopped telling me and maybe I blocked it out and fantasized that he had stopped because I couldn't handle the guilt and pain of knowing that her own father abused her.

That was the last time Chiquis and I really talked about the abuse. I think we were both terribly embarrassed and even though there was some comfort in being able to confide in each other, for many years the memory of that conversation brought me—and continues to bring me—an overwhelming feeling of guilt. I couldn't shake the thought that maybe, just maybe, there was something I could have done to stop Trino from doing what he did to Chiquis. Perhaps if I had just spoken up about it, things might be different. I tossed and turned at night, thinking about how foolish I had been to allow Trino to threaten me into silence. Chiquis and I never discussed any details, but in thinking about the chronology of events, I came to the realization that he had probably started to abuse Chiquis around the time he stopped abusing me. Her nightmare started when mine had finally reached its end.

I thought about something else—to a certain degree my abuse was easier to process: Trino had assaulted me and I could hate him for it. But for Chiquis, it was different. Trino was her father and she loved him. In her eyes, we couldn't tell anyone, not only because of the threats he made (in her case, he threatened to send her away to live with her mean grandmother), but also because this was her father we were talking about, and as much as she hated what he was doing to her, she loved him nonetheless because he was still great to her in many other ways.

Chiquis and I have never discussed any of this, but when I read her book *Forgiveness* and learned the details of what she went through, my heart broke in a million pieces. How she endured all that is unbelievable to me. She is every bit as strong and powerful as her mother, a beautiful, extraordinary soul that no amount of evil or despair will ever crush.

. . .

My depression grew deeper as years went by and I managed to push everyone in my family away. They figured I was going through my rebellious teen years so for the most part, they'd leave me alone. I was so angry, I'd take it out on them but the truth was, I never, ever blamed my parents or my siblings for what happened. My mom and dad were always the most loving, caring parents in the world. They adored me and took care of me in every way they could. They were very involved in all of our lives but when it came to me, probably because I was a girl and the youngest, they always made a huge effort to give me all the time and attention I needed. Yet how did I thank them? By pushing them away and asking them to leave me alone.

My poor parents. They didn't know what to do with me those years when I was so angry. I spoke to them in ways none of my brothers or sister would have ever dared to speak to them. I cursed and yelled, and locked myself in my room for hours at a time. They had no idea how to control this strong-willed, super-intelligent, moody child. By that time I was the only one living at home with them and while I would have never dared to disrespect them if any of my siblings had been around, now that it was just the three of us, I'd lash out at them on any occasion. They loved me so much but I was so different from my older siblings—more "American," less acquainted with the traditional Mexican values of honoring and respecting one's elders—that they simply took a step back and let me be.

One day, my mom and I were on the couch watching an episode of *El Show de Cristina* that was about girls and sex. We were watching in silence but I remember that under the surface, I could feel my blood boil, I was so angry. The way they were discussing the topic was so naive and simplistic and had nothing to do with my experience. It was the confirmation that everything that happened to me was abnormal and I was so angry I felt as if I was going to explode. Suddenly my mother turned to me and asked:

"*Hija,* what do you think about girls who have sex at a young age?"

That's all it took for me to go off on her.

"Why do you ask *me*? Am I supposed to know?" I yelled at her. "Do you think I'm doing it? Leave me alone!" And I just ran into my room and slammed the door.

My poor mother was baffled and I think after that day, she never tried to get close to me again. She never ceased to be there for me, she was always a support, always insisting that I come with her to church, but she no longer tried to get close. I think she shut down because she had never had to deal with anything like this with my older siblings. She simply couldn't believe I'd behave that way.

I felt like a black sheep. No matter where I went, I felt as if I didn't belong. Part of it was the sexual abuse, but part of it was just the way it was, and I think the sexual abuse just emphasized something that was already there. At school I had great grades and I never had a problem with English but the second I said I was Mexican-American, people would smile condescendingly and say, "Oh, *Spanish* is your first language." On the other hand when I went home to Mexico I'd speak Spanish with my cousins but they'd always poke fun at my accent, saying I was a *gringa*. At home, I was a part of this big artistic family but I thought I had a terrible voice and I knew I didn't want to sing. It was as if I was living someone else's life. I didn't fit in so I isolated myself even more: I put up these huge walls and made sure I didn't love anyone *too* much so as not to get hurt. The only person to whom I freely gave my heart was my sister. No matter what happened, no matter how badly I behaved during those terrible teen years—and the years to come—my sister always stood by my side. She never judged me, she never made me feel bad, never ever scolded me. By her side, I always felt accepted, even those times when my parents—whose job it was to discipline and correct me when I was in the wrong—had no idea what to do with me.

It was around the time I turned fifteen that my family started to grow in fame. Lupe was turning into a local celebrity with underground hits like "20 Mujeres" and "El Moreño" and before long the "Rivera Family" became a household name. This brought a sense of prestige and power to our family and while we were all a part of my father and my brother's success, to me it continued to feel as though I was living in the wrong family. They were all so talented and good-looking, so funny and smart. How could I, an overweight, insecure teenager, even be related to them?

Chay had started to record her own music and in addition to his production company, my father was finding success as a recording artist. I was still in high school, yet all of a sudden the world started offering me everything that is supposed to make you happy: money, credit cards, a car, clothes, makeup, you name it. I was spoiled rotten. Feeling ugly? I could go and buy new clothes, get a makeover. Overweight? No problem, I could have surgery to fix it. Yet none of that changed anything I was feeling inside. There was no amount of surgery, clothes, or money that could make me feel better about who I was. I felt only more empty inside.

Dad tried to get me to enter the music world, but I knew it wasn't something I was cut out for like my brothers and sister. I've never wanted to be in the spotlight; I've always felt I had nothing to offer musically. So instead of joining the family business, I started to work in a department store, convinced that if I was able to earn my own money, I'd feel much better about myself, but once again I was wrong.

Everyone knows that in the Mexican-American community turning fifteen is a huge rite of passage. Fifteen is considered to be the year in which girls become women and the affair is marked by a big celebration, similar to a Sweet Sixteen. Girls fret over what dress they're going to wear, who they'll invite, who their *damas* will be, what music will be played. It's a joyous family occasion and everyone north and south of the Río Grande has either had one or been to one.

By the time I turned fifteen, our family was doing well and my father made sure he went all out to make my *Quinceañera* the best.

He rented out the Long Sherman Hall in Wilmington. Wilmington was where my parents lived before I was born, so in a way it was a return to our roots. The Long Sherman was a huge event hall that held about one thousand people and it was a place people used to throw big parties and charge an entry at the door.

"Are you crazy?" I said to my dad when he told me about the location. "How are we going to fill such a big hall? I have no friends!"

I was so antisocial at the time that I really had practically no friends. There was Gladyz and Claudia and maybe two other girls

I was close to, but that was it. I didn't even have enough friends to make the traditional set of seven *damas*, so we had to call in a bunch of cousins I'd barely even talked to, some of whom I didn't even know their names. I didn't know a single boy at the time so someone got me a dude to come out with me and I remember how my brothers were acting all jealous because he happened to be very handsome and he was getting all the attention.

"Don't worry," he said with a big grin on his face. "We'll fill it up." And he sure did. On the day of my *Quinceañera*, my father got on the radio and announced that *anyone* who wanted to come to the party was welcome. *Anyone*. Hundreds and hundreds of people showed up, some with presents, some without, and they were all invited to partake in the festivities. It ended up being a huge mess because some members of my extended family weren't even able to make it in because it was so packed!

And my dad didn't stop there. He already had his recording company so he brought every single band and group he could get. He got Los Canelos, who were really big at the time in L.A., and El Lobito de Sinaloa, who, my father insisted, I loved. (Dad never knew I was in love with Rogelio Martínez.) He also brought Los Razos and Leonel y Amilkar.

I remember begging my father: "Dad, please don't let my brothers get up onstage and sing! I'll be so embarrassed!"

"Ay, *Hija*, don't worry, of course I won't let them sing."

But sure enough, the party started and before too long, my four brothers were up onstage singing. And it was great. The only one who didn't sing that day was Chay, but instead she went up onstage to give a heartfelt speech.

"I want to talk to my sister," she said, and then proceeded to pull out a seven-page letter telling me how much she loved me.

Until that day, I had no idea she felt that strongly. It was a beautiful, emotional moment that I will never forget.

My mother's family had prepared the food and when it was time for dinner, my father said to us, "We're going to serve the guests." So I, in my big white dress, along with my sister, in her fancy dress, my brothers and my parents went around the hall with huge trays of food serving every single person. That was my father's way of saying, no matter how rich or famous you become, you always have to stay humble.

By the time the waltz came around, all I wanted was to be with my whole family, so instead of dancing only with my father or the handsome dude I didn't even know, I wanted everyone to get on the dance floor with their spouse or significant other.

But of course, nothing went as planned. The night before, my sister called me and told me she had gotten into a fight with her husband, Juan.

"Juan is an idiot, so f*** him, he's not coming to your *Quinceañera*, Sister."

"What are we going to do, Sister?" I asked.

"Oh, I have another friend, don't worry."

And sure enough, the next day she showed up with some random guy I'd never even seen before.

"Who's this dude?" I asked her.

"Oh, I'll tell you later, Sister," she whispered.

And that's how it went! We all got out on the dance floor and eventually the whole choreography fell apart and nobody cared. I danced with my father and my brothers and then ended up dancing with Chay (at some point she'd ditched the guy because he couldn't keep up) and all that mattered was that we were all together, surrounded by so much love. By the end of the evening, my face hurt from smiling so much.

It was a beautiful day—a small break from the pain and self-hatred I was going through during those years.

Many years later, my father told me my *Quinceañera* had been one of the happiest days of his life. When I asked him why, he responded: "Because that was the only time I saw you smile for a whole day."

five

the terrifying truth

Three huge events happened when I was sixteen that led me to make a life-changing decision. The first took place at the church our family attended.

One of the members of our congregation was a dearly beloved man, one of those outstanding spiritual people who really knows how to inspire and nurture those around him. He and his wife were admired and respected, not only among the members of the congregation, but also among the community as a whole.

Then some unexpected news hit like a bombshell. A fifteen-year-old in the church confessed that she had been having an affair with the man. The girl felt that she loved him, but at the same time she felt guilty and uncomfortable every time she went to church. The man had started to make her look and feel bad when they were among the congregation and she was confused and didn't understand why he made her feel that way, so she confessed first to her sister in private. The girl was a longtime family friend and we genuinely cared for her, but the prominent member of the congregation was also very important to us, especially because he was a spiritual guide to my brother, Pete.

I felt sick upon hearing this, but there was one thing I desperately needed to find out—when a person like this girl confesses, what would the reaction be? Would people believe her, or would they believe the man? The scandal was far removed from my reality, but in my mind I was contemplating the possible repercussions of revealing something I had never even considered revealing up until then: what if I told the truth about Trino? Would anyone believe me? Or would they believe him?

So as the controversy unfolded, I waited.

The women in our family were shocked and disgusted.

"She's underage!" they'd yell. "This is statutory rape and sexual abuse! Something needs to be done!" I was pleased to hear this, but I still needed to know what the men were thinking—especially my brother Pete, who was the associate pastor of the church.

Pete was upset and very angry at what had taken place. Not only was he shocked like everyone else, but also he was disappointed and felt personally betrayed by his spiritual mentor. With tears in his eyes, he blurted out, "I wish I could break his back!"

He would have never even dreamed of hurting the man, let alone actually physically harming him. But what truly mattered was his reaction, and a wave of relief washed over me when I saw my brother's reaction. He immediately took the young girl's side and insisted that something needed to be done.

Eventually, the man left the church and the girl was vindicated. From that moment forward, a window was open. Maybe, just maybe, I could tell someone what had happened. Trino was no longer a part of the family so the threat of him killing my sister was no longer imminent. Keeping Chay alive had been my priority for so long that I had completely lost sight of what *I* needed and how I could begin to heal. When it came to telling someone about the abuse, my biggest fear had always been that no one would believe me. What happened with that girl in church showed me that things could be different. I saw my family's reaction and their solidarity and compassion made me see something I had never even allowed myself to imagine: maybe my family would be on my side. Maybe they'd help me. Maybe I could be normal again. Maybe my secret wouldn't completely scare them away and maybe, just maybe, they'd still love me.

I lived with those thoughts for a couple of months and it gave me a spark of hope.

The second major event that took place in my life that year also happened at church. I think about it now and I realize how ironic it is that during my teenage years my mother had to literally drag me to church and it was there that I ultimately found my answers.

A guest speaker was visiting our church one Sunday morning and he was particularly interesting because he had what is called "the gift of prophecy"—meaning God reveals certain things to him that He wants people to receive. Not everyone has the gift of prophecy, but the people who have it can guide others into what is going on in their lives, in the present or in the future, based on the Word.

This man didn't know anything about my family, the music industry, and he definitely knew nothing about me. How could he? At that point, I lived in the shadows and as far as I was concerned

I was invisible to the rest of the world. So as usual, I was seated in the very back row of the sanctuary, paying casual attention, but not wanting to be involved in the service.

I perked up, however, when he walked over to my brother Lupe and his wife, María. In front of the entire congregation, the man said, "Be careful with your marriage. It's under attack. Church, just pray for this man and woman."

At the time I knew Lupe and María were having troubles in their marriage; everything he was saying to them was true. I was amazed yet terrified. *Did he also know the truth about what was going on with me? Had God told him my deepest darkest secret?*

Before I knew it, my entire body was shaking. *Please God, don't do this,* I begged. *I'm not ready to talk about what happened. I'm not ready to face this, God! Please, please, give me some more time and let me do it on my own terms,* I pleaded. *Please! Don't let the minister tell the whole church. What if they turn against me? What if no one believes me?*

I was trying my best to fade into the background, but my mother, who had signaled me to sit next to her, kept encouraging me to go down to the front where the visiting preacher was praying with people after his message. It was a very powerful moment and part of me wanted to participate in something so beautiful, but I kept telling myself, *I can't go down there, I just can't!*

Next the preacher asked for those who had dabbled with horoscopes to come forward. I fit that bill, and Mom knew it. But I didn't want to be involved with whatever that man was saying. I was too terrified of what he might know, too scared to hear what he might have to say.

I stayed in the back but the preacher continued.

"There is a young woman here who is hurting terribly. God is calling you. Please come forward. You can feel it inside, and you may be afraid, but God is not going to cause you harm."

Oh, man, I thought. *That sounds like me.* But I refused to budge.

The preacher then called me out. "You, young lady, with the white top and the blue bell bottom pants," he said next. "Please come forward."

I panicked. My first reaction was to turn around and run away as fast as I could but something inside told me I had to stay. My family was there and I could feel their puzzled gazes. *It's now or never,* I thought, and I walked slowly to the front.

Laying his hands on my shoulders, the preacher said, "A spirit of abuse has surrounded your life since you were a little girl. It has saddened and tormented you."

I couldn't believe what he was saying. My entire world had cracked open for everyone to see, and I was too terrified to process what was happening. All I remember was silently pleading with God not to give away Trino's name. *Please, God. Please don't tell them who it is. Please don't say it was Trino.*

I began sobbing uncontrollably. I thought, *This man knows the innermost secrets of my heart, and he is about to reveal the details to everyone.*

Thankfully, God is very gracious and merciful. He knew the exact words to give his prophet. He simply said, "This young woman does not know her value and she has no idea how much she is loved. I beg you, church, show her your love. Hug her and please pray for her life. That's what she needs."

When my family saw me break down in tears, they must have known his words carried some truth, even if they didn't understand what it all meant. At home, I had become so closed off that it was almost impossible for them not to think something serious was going on with me. But they had grown so accustomed to living with my silence and my distance that even after the service, no one tried to get me to open up.

That day, the preacher's words confirmed what I had doubted for so long: I wasn't invisible to God; He hadn't forgotten me or cast me aside. God knew exactly what had happened to me. I didn't know if that made me feel better or worse, but I couldn't help but ask myself, *Does God love me, or is He going to leave me?*

Then the third shoe dropped.

About a month after that Sunday in church, I overheard Chay telling my mother: "I just got into a big argument with Trino and he is threatening to take the children away from me for good. He says I'm on the road too much and he wants to take me to court so he can get full custody."

At the time, Chay was already married to Juan López, and Trino was probably acting up because he was jealous. He couldn't stand to know she had moved on so he did everything he could to make her life miserable. But this was the first time he had threatened to take away the kids.

I knew that if there was one thing Chay was never going to allow was for anyone to mess with her kids. She was a mama before she was anything else and there was no way in hell that she was going to let Trino take her children away from her. But even so, I was terrified. I knew what Trino was capable of and although I assumed that by then he was no longer abusing Chiquis, I couldn't help but worry. What if he had taken it up again? And what about Jacqie—was he abusing her?

It was just too much for me to bear. As scared as I was of telling my sister the truth about what had happened, I was even more afraid of the damage he could continue to do. There was no way I was going to let him take my sister's children away from her and if that meant I had to confront my deepest, darkest demons, then so be it. The crowd reaction to the girl at church as well as the preacher who had been able to read my heart gave me hope that everything would be okay. And even so, I told myself: "I am ready to assume the consequences, even if my family leaves me and the church rejects me. I cannot let Trino take these children."

The final bell rang at Lakewood High and I was walking home. Along the way, on Market Street, were the headquarters of my father's entertainment and music production company, and across the street was my brother Lupe's office, where he had his manufacturing center for CDs. Every single member of our family worked in one of those two buildings—everyone except me.

As I walked, I kept saying to myself, *Rosie, today is the day. You can't put it off any longer. You've just got to do it.* I was planning to tell my sister everything, but I still didn't know how.

When I reached the buildings on Market Street, I walked straight into the office of my brother Pete. I knew Chay would be there—at the time she was working as a secretary in my father's business and she also worked her part-time real estate sales job from that location. Chay was pregnant and in her third trimester with Jenicka. When I reached the building, I caught a glance of her sitting behind the desk with her big belly. Pete's wife, Ramona, was there and she and Chay were engrossed in a deep discussion.

With lead feet, I walked in with my head down, trying my best to act as normal as possible. I have no idea what Chay and Ramona were talking about but I sat down right in front of my sister without even saying "Hello." I stared straight into Chay's eyes and in a flash my sister knew something was terribly wrong. She knew me better than anyone.

Ramona understood something important was going on and she quickly slipped out of the room.

"Sister, you have something to tell me," Chay said to me.

I nodded yes. It was as if she could read my mind.

"Someone has hurt you," she continued.

Again, I nodded.

"It has been going on for a long time, but you're too scared to tell me," she said. "A person has done something to you sexually, right?"

I still hadn't uttered a word. All I had to do was nod yes.

"I want you to know that you can tell me anything. No matter what it is, I'm always going to be with you, Sister. Don't be frightened."

Tears started streaming down my cheeks. My sister, my biggest champion, my best friend, was always going to be with me. How had I ever even doubted that? How could I have let another person's threats come between my sister and me?

"Okay," she continued. "Can you tell me who it is?"

I shook my head and replied, "I can't."

"Can I guess?" she asked calmly.

"Yes," I answered, choking back the tears. So she started guessing.

"Was it one of dad's friends?"

"No," I said.

"Is it someone I know?"

"Yes," I told her.

"Is it a person in the industry?"

I shook my head. Chay guessed a few names but every time I kept shaking my head no.

"I've mentioned every possible name," she finally said. "Why don't you just tell me who it is? Please, Sister, tell me. Who is it?"

I paused for a moment, trying to form the words in my mouth. Finally I was able to whisper: "It is a person very close to you."

In a split second, I could tell that she knew it was Trino. Her eyes grew wide with horror; her mouth opened up in shock. She screamed from the top of her lungs—the loudest scream I have ever heard in my life. It was so loud that my mother, who was in the office across the street, heard it and came running over.

In less than a minute, all four of my brothers were standing in my sister's office. The only member of my family who wasn't there that day was my father, and to this day I don't understand why. He was *always* at the office but that day for some reason he wasn't.

"What in the world is going on?" my brothers asked.

Chay was beside herself. She was on her knees, completely broken, and sobbing uncontrollably. I knelt down on the floor next to her, begging, "Please, please forgive me, Sister! I'm sorry! I'm so sorry!"

Seeing Chay in so much pain was like a dagger piercing through my heart. This was what I had wanted to avoid for years. I had tried to imagine it a thousand times but even so, no amount of imagination could have prepared me for what transpired that day.

With my family huddled over us in total confusion, Ramona explained: "Rosie just told Chay that someone had been sexually abusing her."

Chay turned to our brothers and announced: "Trino."

She managed to calm down, somewhat, and with everyone else there in the room with us, she asked me for details.

"How old were you?"

"I was around eight," I said, wiping back my tears.

"How long did it go on?"

"Until I was about eleven."

Tears stared rolling down her cheeks again.

"God . . . Sister," she muttered. "Why didn't you tell me? All these years . . . Why?"

"I was so scared," I told her. "I was so so scared, Sister. Trino said that if I said anything to anyone, he would kill you and our brothers."

She held me tightly and we both just let the tears flow.

My sister, without any hesitation, automatically believed what I had told her, as did my brothers. In the midst of so much pain and confusion, I once again felt blessed to know I was surrounded by so much love and support. Very upset at what they had just heard, my brothers, in their rage, shouted out, "Let's find Trino."

Pete said, "We have to call the cops," and my other brothers all reluctantly agreed. While one of them dialed the police, I turned to Chay and asked, "Where is Chiquis?"

By my question, she instinctively knew what I was implying, and her face went from pale to green.

"Her too?"

I nodded in tears.

Chay was devastated. She immediately screamed out: "Someone go and get Chiquis. I need to talk to my daughter!"

Chiquis, now twelve years old, was a couple of blocks down the street at the library. When my brothers brought her to the office, she saw us all in tears and right away she knew what was happening.

Remembering the promise we had made each other never to utter a word, I dropped to my knees and begged for her forgiveness: "Baby, I'm so sorry. I had to do it. I had to tell the truth. Please, please forgive me."

Putting on a brave face, Chiquis said to me, "It's okay. It was time. I'm not mad—I just don't want anyone to hurt my daddy."

Within minutes, the police arrived on the scene. In the first phase of their inquiry, they separated us for the questioning. I went first and I remember it was so hard for me to even describe what had happened. I had never spoken to anyone about it and the mere exercise of having to put it all into words made me realize, for the first time, the scope of what had actually occurred. Chay held my hand throughout the whole ordeal, reassuring me and letting me know that I was safe and not alone. As I did my best to recall the most embarrassing details for the sake of the police investigation, I could see the anger rising in her face.

Then it was Chiquis's turn.

Chiquis and I never shared any details but after hearing both sides of the story, my sister now knew everything. Our next step was to take action.

The family devised a plan to pretend that absolutely nothing was going on because, as one of my brothers said, "If Trino hears one word about this, he is going to disappear. He'll run like a scared rabbit and hide."

Chay spoke to the police and they informed her that the next step in the investigation was to bring Chiquis and me in for a medical examination. In the state of California, it's a legal requirement to test all underage children who are victims of abuse. They decided to have Jacqie examined as well. She was eight at the time and given Trino's pattern of abuse, they were concerned that he might have tried something with her.

As soon as the police left, I told Chay, "You need to know that I've had sexual encounters with several other men since then."

She said, "I understand, Sister. It's okay. Everything is going to be okay. I just want you to be well. I promise you we're gonna get you the best counselor out there and you will get through this."

My sister. My big sister. She always stepped up to the plate for me, always believed in me when even I didn't believe in myself. Having her in my corner meant that I could get through this. I knew it.

My biggest concern now was my father. The last thing I wanted was for him to find out about the abuse. I didn't want him to think I was no longer his princess, his precious little girl. I needed him to love me and think I was still amazing and wonderful, that girl who sat on his lap and dreamed of conquering the world.

"Please," I begged my brothers. "Please don't tell Dad. Promise me you won't tell him anything."

"Rosie," said Juan. "No one is going to say a word to him until you tell him yourself."

I nodded, tears rolling down my cheeks. I didn't want to tell him.

"Rosie, you have to tell him," my mother interjected. "You have to tell him tonight."

The entire family gathered around the dining room table. My brothers were there as well as Chay, my mother, and my sister-in-law Ramona. Everyone was tense and my father clearly knew that something strange was going on.

"What is it that you have to tell me, my baby?" he asked.

I was still in shock from what had happened that afternoon. I don't know what words I used; in fact, if I remember correctly I still couldn't bring myself to say anything so someone else had to tell him. Immediately his face got really hard. I took it to mean that he was angry at me, that he was disappointed.

"Why didn't you tell me, *Hija*?" he asked.

"I was too scared, Daddy. I was scared Trino would kill Chay or that my brothers would kill Trino."

I tried to explain the overwhelming fear I had lived with for all those years but my father was tuned out; he went into a type of shock. When you think about it, I had several years to process what had happened to me. I had time to make sense of the horror I lived with for so many years, yet my family had to process it immediately. All those emotions came pouring out and my father's reaction was to shut down.

He asked me a series of very short, quick, questions. And then finally he asked:

"*¿Entonces ya no eres señorita?* (Are you not a virgin anymore?)"

It was such an odd question to ask at a time like that, but later I understood that it was my poor dad's way of asking for details without asking for details.

"No," I answered, and that was the end of the conversation.

At that point Ramona fainted and as soon as she hit the ground, I took advantage of the confusion in order to run away and lock myself in my room. I had been so angry for so many years that everyone knew it was best to leave me alone. And in a situation like this, what could they possibly say to me?

One of the things I love most about our family is that we are all very vocal and we never shy away from speaking our minds. But whenever a situation comes up when we don't have words, we don't just try and fill up the space with unnecessary blabber. If there's nothing to say, there's nothing to say.

. . .

Two days later, Chiquis, Jacqie, and I went to the medical examiner's office. It felt surreal to be talking about and taking such real actions with regard to something I had kept a secret for so long, but with my sister's support, all three of us made it through this difficult experience. In my case, the doctor didn't find any signs of sexual abuse—it had taken place too long ago and I had since been sexually active. But with Chiquis it was another story. She was definitely a virgin, but the doctor found tearing on her vagina—a clear sign of sexual abuse. Little Jacqie had scars as well but fortunately, she had no recollection of the abuse. My sister figured it had probably started when she was very young because she suddenly remembered that when Jacqie was about three years old, she often had a foul odor.

"I think we need to take her to the doctor," Chay would say to Trino. "None of the other babies had this; something is wrong." But Trino always dismissed her worries on account of her being an overprotective mom. On occasion, Jacqie would wet her bed and was unable to stop herself. Poor baby. Whatever it was that Trino did to her must have caused infections that affected her entire body.

To this day, I thank God for having blocked Jacqie's memories of what her father did to her. Despite all the hardship she has had to face from a very young age, she has been able to live a joyful life and her precious spirit has remained intact.

The moment Chay found out about the abuse she vowed never to let Trino near the children again. But since we were waiting for the results of the police investigation, she couldn't actually let him know, yet, why she didn't want them to see him. So she started to make up excuses.

The first excuses didn't raise any alarms, but then Trino started to catch on that something was up. His demands became so intense that when he called, she'd tell him to come by the next day to see the kids, but then when he came by, she made sure they were miles away from the house. There was no way she was going to let him ever come close to them again.

For the first few weeks, Trino would call Chay and threaten her in every way possible. "You're breaking the law!" he'd yell at her. "I'm going to take you to court!"

It was the pot calling the kettle black.

This went on for about a month and then suddenly the phone calls stopped. No more threats, no more demands. Nothing. Chay tried calling him a couple of times just to find out what he was up to, but Trino had vanished. Clearly, he had figured out what had happened and, fully aware of the fact that his actions were punishable by the law, he made sure to fall off the face of the Earth.

Jacqie and Michael, who at the time was just five years old, were terribly confused. They didn't understand why their mother wouldn't let them see their father and worse yet, they didn't understand why their father had disappeared on them like that. They were angry and they blamed Chay for everything they were feeling.

Seeing that Trino had disappeared, Chay tried calling his family and right away she was hit with the confirmation of what we all suspected: Trino was perfectly aware of what was going on because they immediately started insulting Chay and calling her a liar. They said the Rivera family was making up stories about Trino, calling him a pedophile and child molester. "Your brothers are liars and your women are whores," they said to her. "You are nothing but a bunch of opportunists who will do anything for the sake of being in the spotlight."

The names they called us never bothered me. It was clear to us that Trino's family knew where he was hiding but it was also obvious that they were never going to give him up because they believed him. And the truth is, they had every right to believe him because he was their son, their brother, their flesh and blood. If he had been my brother, perhaps I would have believed him too. To this day, I've never been angry at Trino's family because in my eyes they were victims too. They were speaking from a place of ignorance and there was no way they could have ever imagined the truth. Who could have? Even my sister and my family had failed to notice what was going on. With his charming ways and his kind demeanor, Trino had fooled them all.

I didn't need Trino's family to believe me, or anyone else, for that matter. The most important thing was that my family believed me. On top of having to deal with sexual abuse, so many victims have to face the second, and perhaps harsher reality, of not being believed by their loved ones. I cannot imagine the despair that must cause and I am thankful for having always had a supportive family who never questioned a single thing I told them.

Having lost touch with Trino and given the fact that his family was never going to tell us where he was, we were entirely in the hands of the detectives from the Long Beach Police Department. They assured us that they were working on the case, and we felt confident that Trino would be found and brought to justice.

A year passed.

Then two.

Chay would phone for an update and the department would reassure her, "We're on it." But before long, they stopped returning her calls.

· · ·

One night our family was having a barbecue at Chay's house. Everyone was there except Lupe, who was running late. We didn't want to start eating without him so we called him several times on his cell phone but there was no answer, so we sat down to eat.

A couple of hours later, Lupe finally arrived and we could tell he was really upset.

"You'll never believe it," he told us as he sat down in front of a plate of cold food. He looked angry. "I just spotted Trino on the 710 freeway. I know it was him, and I'm convinced he saw me."

"WHAT?" we all asked in unison. We couldn't believe it. By then we had all assumed he was hiding somewhere out of the country. To hear that he was in our vicinity both terrified me and filled me with hope.

"Well, I started after him and it turned into a high-speed chase," he told us. "I didn't care what was going to happen; I only knew that if I caught that piece of sh*t I was going to kill him. But I lost sight of his car."

Lupe was angry that the cops hadn't been able to find Trino, and now he had slipped through his fingers too. I had never seen my brother so furious. The barbecue took second place while we rehashed what we had just heard. We decided that more so than the fact that he had gotten away, the important piece of news was that Trino was still in the area. We all assumed he had fled to Mexico, but Chay remembered that Trino had once confided in her that when he was young he had been kicked out of his hometown. He never gave her any details but it had always stuck with her. Why couldn't he go back? We started putting two and two together and wondered whether he was guilty of a similar charge in his native country.

Frustrated that the police were making absolutely no effort to track him down, my brothers decided to take matters into their own hands. They started spreading the word around the neighborhood, showing pictures and asking friends, and friends of friends, whether they had seen Trino.

That was how we found out that there were a few guys in our part of town who were in touch with Trino. Word on the street was that he had changed his name and hangouts and remarried and had children before he became a fugitive. Apparently he had also gotten a nose job, dyed his hair, and changed his appearance to look much younger.

A tip led us to the information that Trino had been invited to a certain party. My brothers decided to go—and bring Chiquis and me along. They also bought along some of the guys who knew him so they'd be able to identify him.

At the party, I saw my brothers huddled in a corner talking to a few men who looked dangerous and probably carried guns. We sat around at the party and while everybody else seemed to be having a good time, to Chiquis and me, every second that went by seemed like an eternity. We were terrified for Trino's life. Yes, I wanted justice for his actions, but not like this. If he was shot and killed, my brothers would probably go to jail and Chiquis would be left without a dad. In our heart of hearts, we both still felt that Trino wasn't a bad or evil person; we were convinced that he needed help.

Chiquis and I huddled together and prayed: "Please, God, don't let them find Trino. Please don't let him show up."

And he didn't.

Over time, the pressure to find Trino became a huge burden on my soul. Every January, when the time for New Year's resolutions came around, my dad would always say to me: "This is the year we catch Trino, *Hija.* This is the year we find him."

As time passed, my father's prediction made me more and more anxious. I knew my dad was just trying to motivate me, and he probably was doing the same with my brothers, but I was still afraid of what would happen if they ever found Trino. More important, all I really wanted was to put the whole episode behind me. I wanted to move on with my life; I wanted to live in a world free from the shadow of Trino. The fear and uncertainty of not knowing whether he was around the corner or on the run in some far-away part of the country was eating me up inside. It felt as if the weight of the world was resting on my shoulders.

six

downward spiral

After my confession, I went completely nuts. There's no other way to put it. I had lived with my secret for so long that as soon as I let it out into the world, all hell broke loose. Far from bringing me peace and comfort, the truth had blown my life up into a thousand pieces and I had no clue how to put it back together.

On the day I told her about Trino, my sister said she would help me get all the counseling and the therapy I needed to get over what had happened. And as always, she kept her promise. I met with all sorts of experts on depression, sexual abuse, addiction, and during our sessions, I truly understood and believed what they told me: the abuse isn't your fault, you are worthy of love, it's normal to be angry, it's normal to feel scared.

But once I left the safe confines of their offices, I was thrown back into a harsh world that kept telling me that nothing about me was normal. I hated myself, I hated my life—I didn't know who I was anymore and all I wanted was to escape. Every day, from the moment I got up in the morning to the moment I went to sleep, I walked around like a zombie, hoping to be put out of my misery.

I started drinking when I was about thirteen years old and by the time I was eighteen, I had to start the day with a shot of tequila. Before too long, I added drugs to the mix and not a day went by without taking something. I'd hide in the high school bathrooms and get high on just about anything I could get my hands on. First cocaine, then marijuana, and eventually I graduated to Ecstasy. The cycle was always the same. As soon as I took the drug, I felt as if I was soaring on top of the world and numb to the pain, and while I knew all the stress of my daily life was still tucked inside, the drugs allowed me to put it on hold for a moment. I loved how light and carefree they made me feel but as soon as the drugs wore off, I was left feeling scared and guilty, promising myself to never do it again. But then I would, and the vicious cycle would start all over again.

Now that I had told my family about Trino's abuse, they finally understood the reasons for my behavior, but that didn't mean it made things any better. I was still difficult and abrasive, and no matter how hard they tried, I did everything in my power to keep them at bay.

I knew that if my grades started to drop my parents would get on my case so I made sure I stayed a straight-A student all the way through high school and college. As long as my grades were good, they figured I couldn't be doing *too* badly, so for the most part they'd let me be, and that was exactly what I thought I needed.

Sexual abuse messes with you on so many levels. There are the psychological effects, of course, of feeling dirty and rejected, but there is also a physical component. Your body is introduced to sex at such a young age that you're not yet ready to process it emotionally. Deep down, I was a hopeless romantic. I wanted so desperately to find love and for it to make me feel good, protected and cared for. The problem was, I didn't love myself; so how could I expect anyone to love me? I still thought that the only way to find love was through sex.

When I was seventeen years old, I started dating Luis, a boy I met at the Música del Pueblo store my dad owned in Huntington Park. I was working the cash register and he would come in and buy CDs every week just to say hello. He was short, dark, and attractive, funny and a family guy. But what I liked most about him was that he was three years older and that meant he was more mature than any of the guys my age. A month went by and I was crazy in love.

Luis and I were having sexual relations, but I was taking precautions so I wouldn't become pregnant. Since killing Trino wasn't an acceptable option, I had my mind set on going to law school and becoming an attorney to find justice. I didn't want anything to distract me from my plan, and an unplanned pregnancy certainly wasn't something I was going to allow.

Well, something must have gone wrong, because one day I started feeling nauseous and woozy. The discomfort lasted for a couple of days before I realized that not only was I feeling ill, but my period was late. *No way!* I thought, somewhat panicked. *Could I be pregnant?* I had to know right away so I rushed out to the drugstore and bought myself a pregnancy test.

I followed the instructions, and three minutes later I had my answer: I was pregnant.

Like in most of the defining moments of my life, I was alone. Yes, a baby wasn't in my plans but I couldn't help smiling as the tears rolled down my face. Maybe this baby was going to be the one to turn my life around. Would Luis marry me? Did this mean I was finally going to have a normal life? I knew in my heart that I wanted a career and I wanted Trino behind bars, but the fleeting illusion of everything finally being okay was a powerful temptation.

I told Luis the news and like me, he was terrified at the thought of becoming a parent. He couldn't wrap his mind around what was happening. He kept saying: "This can't be true. This can't be happening. I'm not ready to be a father!"

And I wasn't any more ready to be a mother. I was completely lost. Having a baby meant that all my hopes for the future were, once again, going to be crushed. While my life had been a huge mess since the abuse happened, the one thing I always held on to, the one thing I always excelled at was school, because I knew it was the key to my future. Even through my darkest times, I'd managed to keep up my good grades and that was a source of pride for me. In fact, I had my heart set on going to college and eventually becoming an attorney like Marcia Clark, who I'd seen on TV during the O.J. Simpson trial. I wanted to be just like her—a woman attorney—except I'd win the case and bring justice. She was the first woman trial lawyer I had ever seen and I thought she was bold and cool, crazy hair and all.

But it didn't take too much to understand that with a baby, all those dreams would never come true. I'd have to drop out of school in order to raise my child, and who knew what would happen then? I'd probably end up being just another statistic. And there was nothing I hated more than that prospect.

Days went by and Luis and I discussed our options but we never seemed to get to any sound conclusion. We kept going round and round in circles. What were we going to do? I was broken and depressed and clearly wasn't equipped to be facing such a momentous decision. Luis grew more and more impatient with me and before too long he started to threaten me: "If you have this baby, I am going to say it's not mine," he'd say. "It will be the shame of your family because everyone will know you had a child out of wedlock."

I knew what it would mean for my parents to have a grandchild born out of wedlock and as understanding as they had always been with me, that was something I didn't want to put them through. They had given me everything a girl could possibly dream of and I wasn't ready to dump yet another problem on their laps. All the drama surrounding the abuse had been more than enough.

Finally, Luis gave me an ultimatum: either I went to get an abortion, or he would leave me right then and there. I loved Luis, and I didn't want him to leave—I already had abandonment issues and didn't want to be shunned again. But I also didn't want to get an abortion. I might have found myself far away from God at that point in my life, but I was well aware that killing is a sin and I certainly didn't want to kill my own baby. I was so terrified of the situation that I was incapable of processing a rational thought: all I wanted was to get Luis to stay with me, and not have to put my family through shame. Soon enough, I came to what seemed like the only viable solution.

I found the name and location of an abortion clinic, and Luis and I decided to go there without telling a soul. I thought that if no one found out, I could stick to my plans, avoid disgracing my family, and get on with my life.

That day, before we drove to the clinic, I locked myself in the bathroom and listened to "Reloj" by Luis Miguel on repeat, praying that time would stop so I could spend just a little more time with my unborn child, Esperanza Soledad. I wanted to say good-bye before I even had the chance to see her face, treasuring that precious moment with her.

It was another beautiful and perfect Southern California day and the Planned Parenthood clinic was in Los Angeles so Luis drove me there early in the morning. There were no jokes, no music playing in the background—we drove in absolute silence, each of us lost in our own thoughts. I remember I rode the whole way facing the passenger window so Luis couldn't see the tears rolling down my face—the last thing I wanted was to make him upset. I wanted to seem brave and sure of this decision, but in my heart I hoped he would suddenly turn the car around and take me to his mother's house in South Central so that we could raise our baby and be together forever. I walked through the doors with a lump in my throat and heaviness in my heart. My mind had made the decision to be there, but every cell in my body was telling me to leave. As I filled out the paperwork, my emotions swung back and forth like a pendulum. Was I doing the right thing? Should I go through with this, or should I run out the door? Would God punish me for being so selfish?

I signed my name and handed the receptionist the paperwork before taking a seat in the waiting room. Before long, a medical assistant came to get me and I followed her into a small, private room.

I was given a sedative and as I drifted in and out of consciousness the doctor started to ask me some personal questions, perhaps because she was looking to put my mind at ease.

"Have you ever been under general anesthesia?" she asked. "Did you eat anything this morning? Don't worry, honey, this will be fast and you'll be able to go home and move on with your life in no time."

Move on with my life? What life? I felt so selfish. This child already had a life and I was taking it.

Tears rolled down my cheeks.

"Please!" I suddenly shouted. "Please stop! I've changed my mind. I don't want to go through with this! I want to keep my baby!" But I was already beginning to fall into a deep sleep. The last thing I remember was looking at her stern face and then the blinding light on the ceiling that I hoped would turn into the light at the end of life's tunnel. I hoped with all my heart that I wouldn't have to wake up again.

When I opened my eyes, I asked the nurse: "Did you go through with it? Please tell me I didn't kill my baby. Please tell me you heard me when I asked you to stop."

But it was too late. The doctor had performed the abortion and there I was, bleeding and in so much pain, ashamed that I had been so selfish. Was this what my parents had taught me? I couldn't believe that I had wanted a career more than a child. "Family comes first," is what my father had always taught us, and that day in the abortion clinic, I failed miserably to live up to the values he had instilled in me.

After spending some time in the recovery room, the nurse informed me that it was time for me to go home. Before I left, she handed me some medication, saying that I needed to take it in order to avoid getting an infection.

Little did the nurse know that instead of giving me a warning to stay safe, she had given me a way to punish myself. My immediate thoughts were, *I don't care if I get an infection; in fact I would be thrilled to get one. If I'm lucky enough, maybe I will even die! That's what I deserve for being such a self-centered, monstrous human being.*

By the time I got home, I was feeling so terrible that all I wanted was to hole myself up in my room and cry until I had no more tears left. I dropped the pills and the paperwork on the dining room table and quickly went to my bedroom before I crossed paths with anyone—the last thing I wanted was to have to answer any questions.

While I was sleeping in my bedroom, my mother found the medicine and paperwork on the dining room table and immediately turned them over to Brenda, my brother Juan's wife, for translation. It was careless of me to leave the paperwork there but maybe it was a subconscious act, maybe part of me really wanted to be found out.

My long-suffering mother wasn't about to let this one go. Yes, she had kept quiet about me dating too many boys and drinking too much alcohol, but this wasn't something she could ignore. It went against everything she believed in, everything she stood for. The baby I was carrying was *her* grandchild and I had had no right taking him or her away from her.

That evening, as soon as I peeked my head out of my bedroom door, my mom came rushing over, with the bottle of pills in her hand.

"What are these?" she asked me, furious.

"How am I supposed to know?" I answered, trying to act indifferent.

"What do you mean you don't know, *Hija*? It says here that these are antibiotics and that you had an abortion today," she continued. "*Dios bendito,* what in the world were you thinking, Rosie?"

The sadness in her eyes broke my heart. Yet even though I was just as appalled as she was, I wasn't ready to let her into my innermost thoughts. As I had done so many times in the past, when the truth was looking me square in the eyes, I built a wall of anger and refused to let anyone in.

"I don't care what you think. This is *my* life and *my* body. Stay out of my business!"

All I wanted was for her to leave me alone. Not only was I grieving for my lost child. I could tell by the look on her face that I had also broken her heart, and that was too much for me to bear. I knew she didn't care whether I got good grades or became some hotshot attorney. All she cared about was her family and she was distraught over what I had done.

"You know God doesn't allow this!" she screamed, her voice shaking with sorrow and disbelief.

"Well, I don't care what God thinks!" I answered, and I went back to lock myself up in my room.

Luis and I dated for three months, on and off. We never talked about the incident again, and neither did my mother and I. It was as if it had never happened. I acted as though I'd moved on when in fact not a day goes by that I don't think about my baby in Heaven.

At Lakewood High, during my senior year, I was active in several organizations, president of the Hispanic Los Amigos Club, member of the student council, and one of the speakers at the 1999 graduation. Classmates and teachers I hardly knew came up to me that day and said, "Rosie, we are proud of you. We know you are going to have a fantastic future."

I wore my best smile and thanked them, but inside I thought, *If they only knew.*

After high school, I got my first liposuction—another attempt at making myself thin and beautiful in order to find love, marriage, and happiness. Somehow I thought it would be the miraculous solution to all my problems. Needless to say, it wasn't.

I enrolled at the University of California, Irvine. Because I had to drive there every day, my dad gave me my first car and to me that meant freedom! I was still living at my parents' house but I could go anywhere I wanted at any time of the day and night.

I chose Criminology as my major because I was still set on becoming an attorney. The Trino situation still haunted me and I wanted to work in a profession that would allow me to put him—and anyone else like him—behind bars.

During my college years, I spent a lot of time with my sister at her house in Compton, where she lived with her five kids. By then, she had probably separated from Juan because I remember we had a lot of fun, and my sister was *always* more fun when she was single.

Every morning we'd wake up and Chay would get the kids ready. Chay would rush off to work and then I'd take my morning shot of tequila and drive myself to school. I wasn't drunk, but it felt good. I wanted to be a little numb in order to face the day ahead.

I'd spend the day at school going to classes and lectures, doing homework, studying in the library. I didn't want anyone to notice me so for the most part I kept to myself and at the end of the day, I'd get behind the wheel of my car and drive back home to Chay's house or my parents' house.

During the weekdays, I was really good. I'd stay focused on school, making sure, as always, that my grades didn't lag. But come Friday, when all my work was done, I would go all out. I would go clubbing, hang out with friends, and if for some reason my friends were busy, I would go get drunk by myself. I'd get all dressed up to go to these trashy little clubs with the sole purpose of getting super wasted and maybe finding someone to sleep with.

At that point, all I wanted was to die. Yes, I loved my family;

yes, I wanted a career, but if I had been faced with the prospect of leaving this Earth right then and there, I would have taken it in a minute. In addition to the scars left behind by the abuse, I carried around with me the pain of having had that abortion and all I wanted was to punish myself for what I had done. I tried everything I could in order to get someone to kill me without having to kill myself: I'd wear really skimpy clothes, go to seedy clubs all by myself, drive drunk, and talk to any guy that would talk to me, just in case he wanted to do something to me and then get rid of me, hoping no one would ever find out. I'd make sure to change my name and hide my cell phone so no one could reach me. I'd put myself in extremely dangerous situations; I slept with so many men that I'm ashamed to say I can't even remember their names. I didn't care who they were or what they did to me; the only thing driving me was an intense desire to disappear.

Every Friday it was the same thing: I'd go out, party hard, come back home to sleep, and head back out to another club on Saturday and Sunday. For the most part, I did this when I was staying at Chay's house and although she never judged me or made me feel bad for what I was doing, I know she definitely worried.

"Sister, you need to be more careful," she'd say to me. "Don't take anyone's drink. Don't sleep around! You *need* to take care of yourself. I know you do these things because of the sexual abuse and that's why I don't judge you, but you have to be careful or else one day you're not going to be okay . . . And I *need* you to be okay, Sister."

That's how it always went between us. Since I had spent so many years fearing for her life, I would say to her, "Sister, I need you to live," and she would say to me, "Sister, I need you to be okay."

"I know why you do this, I know why you drink, I know why

you are promiscuous, Sister," she'd continue. "I understand, and I'm waiting for you to get through it. You'll get through it, Sister. I know it."

We'd have these long conversations and she would always be so good to me, so understanding, so loving. She never made me feel as if there was something wrong with me as a person. She let me know my actions were wrong, but she still loved me and was understanding, giving me her full support. "You have so much potential," she'd say to me. "You can really be somebody! Sister, you should be in front of the camera as a reporter or doing the weather. You should have your own show one day!"

"You're nuts!" I'd say. "Can't you see that I'm a mess?"

"You're a mess right now, Sister, but you're the greatest person I know," she'd answer. Then she would flash me one of her beautiful Chay smiles and there was so much conviction in her words that sometimes I almost believed her. I certainly *wanted* to believe her. During those challenging years, Chay gave me so much attention and love. She was my only source of comfort when everything was dark. I don't know that I would have survived through it all without her.

By the end of our conversations, I always felt stronger and determined to make a real change in my life. I had great parents, a great family that had worked its butt off as immigrants to get us to where we were. I had every single opportunity to be a good person: a good citizen, a successful career, whatever I set my mind to, I knew I could accomplish. Then how could I waste my life away like that? *I have to be a better Rosie for Chay,* I'd say to myself. *This is the last time I do this. This is the last weekend I go out like this. It's the last time.*

But then I'd have trouble falling asleep so I thought, *I'm just going to have one drink—just one drink to help me sleep better.*

But inevitably one drink would become two, and three, and four, and before long, I was back to square one: the weekend came around and all I wanted to do was let loose and leave all the pain behind.

All those years, Chay never lost faith in me, and neither did my mother. She never stopped believing in me, never gave up on getting me to come back to church and embrace God. I'd come home at four o'clock in the morning, super drunk and wearing the shortest skirt ever. God knows where I had been. I'd stumble through the door, and there was my mom, patiently waiting for me on the sofa with curlers in her hair and wearing her little *batita* with no bra on. As soon as I saw her, I would get *so* upset, *so angry* when she'd ask me where I'd been.

"Why don't you go to sleep?" I'd yell at her. "What do you care what I'm doing?"

I thought I was so tough. I had been through a lot, from being made fun of for being dirty at the swap meet, to being fat and broke, to being sexually abused, to having had an abortion and doing all sorts of drugs. I felt that there was nothing my mom could say to make things better. *I am so much stronger than you, lady,* I thought. *Don't worry about me. Getting home at four in the morning is nothing! Can't you see nothing is going to happen to me, lady?* Little did she know I was actually *trying* to kill myself but no matter how hard I tried, nothing ever happened. I never used condoms; I drank from anyone's drink; several times I had tried to overdose on drugs and pills but nothing ever happened to me. I was never in a car accident, never got an STD, nothing. Getting home at four in the morning was nothing.

"Just leave me alone and go to sleep! *Déjeme en paz!*" I'd

scream at her as I walked down the hallway to my room. She'd follow me, saying, "*No, Hija, las señoritas decentes no llegan a estas horas.* Decent girls don't come home at this hour."

"I'm not a decent woman, *Mamá*!" I'd yell back at her. "Don't you understand? I don't care! This is my life and I'm never going to be a decent woman so why don't you just leave me alone?"

I'd go into my room and she'd walk in right behind me.

"No, Rosie, I refuse to believe—"

"*Ay, Ma, ya cállese!* Shut up!"

"No! I'm not going to shut up! I'm not going to leave you alone! I'll never get tired of telling you that you're going to be a good woman! God loves you and you need to change. You will change!"

"I don't want to change!" I'd scream back at her. "And I don't want to go to your stupid church!" I was so angry. I genuinely didn't know why she cared and why she couldn't just let me be.

I'd lie down on my bed, pretending to be asleep, and my mother, all tiny and chubby, so adorable in her *batita* and her rollers, would put her hands on me. She'd rub my legs with anointing oil as she began calling out to God what she saw with her spiritual eyes and heard with her spiritual ears—and I listened to every word.

"Rosie," she'd say, speaking softly and tenderly, "you are a great woman of God. You will sing and speak for Him. My Lord will win this battle. I declare that you will be healed and liberated from all these demons that torture you."

As far-fetched as her words seemed to me, I couldn't help but admire her faith. To this day, it's one of the things I admire most about my mother. She was going against everything she saw, everything she heard and everything she knew. I was the exact opposite of everything she was saying yet she never lost faith in what God can accomplish. She knew it would take a miracle for me to become the woman she wanted me to be.

I looked up at my mom as she turned to leave my room and I felt sorry for her and unworthy. It all seemed ridiculous, pathetic to such a point that I wasn't even angry anymore. *Mi pobre Mami,* I thought. *She doesn't deserve to have me as a child. She deserves so much better.*

My dad, in the meantime, never said a word to me. Since the day he found out about the sexual abuse, he didn't know what to do with me. He didn't know what to say. As a father, he felt he was supposed to be my protector and I think he probably felt as if he'd failed, as if he had lost all credibility with himself.

But to me it was all the same. In my eyes he was just another person I had managed to alienate from my life, and I was actually glad he left me alone.

That said, deep down in my heart I knew my father enough to know he was disappointed in me—both of them were. And it wasn't just the fact that I had strayed away from God. It had more to do with my lack of values and self-respect. What mattered to them most in life was having values—your respect for yourself and your respect for your family. Yes, I was getting good grades and was on my way to becoming a hotshot attorney, but none of that mattered if I didn't have the right values. The reality was that I didn't love myself and I didn't respect my family, and no matter how much I tried to hide behind my supposed accomplishments, I knew it was all just a facade.

My parents weren't the only ones who knew about my risky behavior. My extended family and other people in the community never said anything to my face but they'd tell my mother.

"Rosie, people tell me that you are a lost cause, *eres una causa perdida,*" she'd say to me. "They tell me that you are uncontrollable and you'll never amount to anything. They say you'll probably end up a single mom, broke, and addicted to drugs. That's what they tell me, Rosie. That's what they say."

She'd tell me this not because she wanted to hurt me, but because she was trying every single way to get me to react. She tried the nice way, the screaming way, the you-can't-do-this-in-my-home way. She tried taking me to therapy, to church, anything and everything that could help. And she never gave up.

"*Hija*, you know God loves you," she'd say to me.

"Whatever with God, Mom," I'd mumble back. "He doesn't care about me."

"No, *Hija*, you don't understand. God loves you just as you are."

"He can't possibly love me," I'd answer. "Not after having an abortion."

"But, *Hija*, He will forgive you."

"Mom, I'm not sorry about it."

It was a blatant lie, of course, but at that point I'd say just about anything to get her off my case. Yet my mother would never give up. Never. She invited me to go to church with her every weekend even though I'd gripe and complain. "They're all hypocrites. Look what church leaders and other people do. I'm better off out in the clubs."

"You're wrong if you think you can survive this difficult life on your own, Rosie. There's a war going on between good and evil, and—"

"Look, Mom," I'd interrupt her. "You don't understand who I am. The church will refuse me as soon as I show up drunk or smelling of alcohol. What if I smoked a cigarette outside?"

"Daughter," she'd respond, "you haven't understood a word I've been saying. I don't care how you show up for church or what people think. It's not the church that receives you, but the Lord. The doors are open for everyone—from the prostitute on the street to the town drunk."

"Whatever," I answered, and let her ramble on.

Then she said something I've never forgotten: "Jesus has His arms wide open—the way He was on the cross."

seven

toxic love

Just when I thought there was absolutely no hope left for me in the world, a handsome young man came along. I'll call him Chief.

I was twenty, in my junior year at college and we met at El Rodeo, a nightclub in Pico Rivera, the same place where Chay talked to the love of her life, Ferny, for the first time. I was off to the side watching Chay run the stage as if she had been born on it, when I heard a guy say my name.

I turned around and saw a handsome twenty-something motioning for me to dance. I never liked dancing when my sister was onstage so I made a sign with my index and thumb saying "in a little bit," as I winked and smiled back at him. From where I was standing I could tell he was tall—taller than Luis, at least, and that was a plus—dark and handsome. I liked what I saw.

As soon as the Diva finished her set, I walked over to him and asked him, straight out, how he knew my name.

"Everyone here knows who you are, Rosie: Lupillo and Jenni's little sister," he said with a grin on his face.

I was surprised because at the time I didn't even realize people knew I existed. I didn't like knowing that people watched me or knew anything about my life through the media since eighty percent of the time they're lying and the other twenty percent are conveniently "bending" the truth. I felt uncomfortable that he was a fan but he was too cute to let go so I let it pass. I didn't end up dancing with him that night, but we did chat for a little while, and then we exchanged phone numbers.

Chief and I went on a few dates and right away we clicked. It was an immediate connection. After the first few weeks of dating, we told each other that we were in love. (He said it first, actually. I was much too scared of rejection to ever say it first.) He was so attentive, romantic, manly, and intelligent that I was convinced that I had found the love of my life. And to top it all off, he loved baseball, just like the other guys in my family! What wasn't there to love? No one had ever made me feel that way before and I knew for sure that we were meant to be together. I wanted our relationship to last so one day I told him what was in my heart.

"I'm not here to play," I said. "I want something serious."

"I'm not either," he replied. "I love you."

For years, I had been stumbling from one disappointing relationship to another, so to finally hear someone tell me that he loved me felt like balm for my soul.

Chief made me feel loved and slowly but surely, I started to calm down. I practically stopped drinking and doing drugs because Chief thought it wasn't ladylike, and because I wanted to become his lady, I started to change. It was an extremely positive turn for me at the time, but even so, my family wasn't entirely on board with Chief. They liked the changes they were seeing in me but Lupe and Mom, for example, had a bad feeling. They thought that Chief would eventually hurt me and they kept telling me to be careful. Lupe, whose opinion on guys I valued above anyone else's, told me I should leave him. Normally that would have been enough to make me drop the relationship in a heartbeat, but this time I was so in love that I didn't listen to him. Seeing how important Chief was to me, Lupe eventually gave us his blessing and promised to support me as long as Chief respected his home.

As our relationship evolved, we started to talk about the future. We knew we wanted to spend the rest of our lives together but we were in no rush. We were both very serious about our careers— I was going to finish college and then apply to law school—and he was working up the management ladder at a large retail store. I felt lucky to be with a man who respected and supported my aspirations and I was going to make sure I respected his.

Having sex before marriage was the norm for both of us, but we didn't use protection; we decided the "pull out" method would work just as well. For the first time since Luis, I was having sex with someone I actually loved, and everything about our relationship felt right. I was happy. After so many years of trauma, I was finally feeling good about myself—I had a good man by my side who made me feel like a million bucks.

Things were running along smoothly until about nine months into our relationship, we had our first argument. I wanted to go to a concert with a couple of my girlfriends but when I told him about my plans, he simply said, "No."

Granted, in the Mexican-American community, a concert means a music performance at a big nightclub where there is drinking and dancing, but I had been going to concerts all my life (my family was in the music business!) and I wasn't going to stop just because my boyfriend said so. I'd spent so many years disobeying every rule my parents gave me—why was I going to start obeying his?

A huge fight ensued and I ended up breaking up with him and going to the concert. He asked me to get back together with him a couple of weeks later but I played hard to get even though deep down we both knew I'd come back.

For a few weeks, he'd call and text me all the time. "Hey, baby. I miss you. Why don't you come over and be with me again?"

At the beginning I didn't respond, but soon enough his sweet messages broke me down and we ended up seeing each other again. We didn't go back to being in a committed relationship but we did get together from time to time to have sex.

In my family, there are three important holidays that I would never miss for anything in the world: Thanksgiving, Christmas, and July Fourth. We celebrate the Fourth of July not just because it's Independence Day, but because Chay and I have birthdays around that date and we always celebrated our birthdays together. I was born on July third, and Chay came into the world on July second—so we always threw a big bash on the fourth. This time we were having it at our brother Lupe's house.

As always, it was a great party. There's nothing I love more than spending time with my family and that July Fourth was no exception. I was turning twenty-one and Chay was turning thirty-three so we went all out. My whole family was there and some of their famous friends, but no one was acting rich or famous— we were just having a blast, eating carne asada and downing Coronas. Lupe's house is a gorgeous three-story home in Playa del Rey, and that night we were able to see the romantic fireworks over Marina del Rey.

At the last minute, I decided to invite Chief to come along, because he knew my family and he was, I guess, the closest thing I had to a boyfriend. We were drinking and dancing and having a great time. Chief and I stepped out to the front of the house to get some air when suddenly I noticed I had a voice mail on my phone. It was from a guy I knew casually; he was probably just calling to say happy birthday or something. I put the phone up to my ear to listen to the message but before I was able to do so, Chief grabbed the phone from my hand to listen to the voice message.

Seriously? Who did he think he was?

"You are not my boyfriend anymore, and you don't have a right to do this!" I yelled while I snatched the phone back from him.

Without a second of hesitation, he slapped me across the face.

I couldn't believe what he had done. God knows I had been in some pretty bad situations in my life, but no one had ever hit me before. As Daddy said, "No one touches Rosie." I was furious but for the sake of not creating a scene, I was able to take a step back.

"You are a very lucky man," I said to him. "I don't like drama around my family and I'm not about to call the cops and ruin this party, but you need to leave right now."

I knew that if my brothers found out that he had slapped me they would have beat him right then and there. So practically pushing him off the front porch, I said to him, "I never want to see you again. Just get out of my face and out of my life—and don't ever come back."

After he left, I went back inside and joined the rest of the party in downing shots, acting as if nothing was wrong. I was shaken and upset, but no one noticed anything strange, of course, since by then, I knew perfectly well how to hide my feelings.

What I *didn't* know was that Chief hadn't actually left the party. He just waited outside for a while before coming back in. Then, from across the big room upstairs, I heard him call: "Hey, baby, come here. Let's talk. I want to—"

Whatever it was he was going to say, I didn't want to hear it.

"Get out of here," I hissed. "Get out of this house."

He refused. He just hung around, glaring at me from a distance, probably just waiting for me to get really drunk. And sure enough, I did. With every shot, I grew weaker and more vulnerable. I couldn't handle having him standing around looking at me, so after a while I walked over to him to find out what it was he wanted.

"I just want to talk to you," he said sweetly.

He took me by the hand, led me into a bathroom downstairs and locked the door behind us. I must have blacked out because the next thing I remember is waking up on the floor of that bathroom, half naked and confused. It was obvious that we'd just had sex. I looked over at Chief as he was pulling up his pants and said, "Wait, I need to clean up. Where did you finish?"

"Inside of you," he answered.

I was confused and furious. This had never happened with us before.

"What? That's wrong!" I blurted. "It's my body and you have no right to treat me this way!"

The last thing I needed was to get pregnant again. My sights were set on completing college, going to law school, and continuing my quest to put Trino behind bars. If I got pregnant, none of that would be possible, especially since I had promised myself that I'd never have an abortion again.

A weird grin crept over his face and he said: "Well, now you know you're mine. If you're pregnant, you won't be able to leave me ever again because the baby will be ours together."

That's how I knew he'd planned it all along.

Sure enough, a few weeks later, I started to feel sick and exhausted all the time. At first I tried to dismiss it but when my mom made a passing comment about how late I was sleeping and how little I was eating, I pretty much knew what was going on. I was terrified. So I called Chief and said, "Hey, it's Rosie. We need to go to Planned Parenthood."

"What for?" he asked.

"I think I'm pregnant and need to find out for sure."

"Oh, well, that's your problem," he snapped back.

"What do you mean? Are you saying you changed your mind?" I asked in disbelief. Was this the same man I'd last spoken to?

When I reminded him of what he had said in the bathroom at Lupe's house, about how he planned this so we would always be together, he just flippantly responded, "Yeah, well . . . I changed my mind."

"No!" I protested. "I don't care whether you changed your mind. I need you to go to the clinic with me to find out for sure if you are going to be a father."

After some back and forth, he finally agreed. "Okay, I'll go, but you are just being dramatic; you're not really pregnant."

I certainly hoped he was right.

We drove to the clinic but because we weren't married, they wouldn't let him come into the examination room with me. I went through the test alone.

When I walked out to the lobby, he looked at me expectantly.

"I was right," I told him. "I'm pregnant."

There was no smile, no hug, no tears of joy.

"Well, I'm sure you're going to call a press conference and make a big deal out of it," he said. "That's what you and your family always do."

"Well, you're wrong. That's not how I'm going to handle it," I said, when in fact I had no idea how I was going to handle anything. I was lost and scared, and all I wanted was to go and tell my big brother Lupe. He would know how to take care of me.

"I'm going to go see Lupe," I said after a brief pause. "Will you come with me?" I asked.

"No way," he answered, giving me the sense that that was where he drew the line. "But I have a message for Lupe and your family. Tell them I'm not going to marry you."

"That fine," I replied, trying my best to stay calm.

"And tell them I don't want to be with you anymore—and I'm not going to move in with you."

"That's fine, too," I answered. I was too confused to argue.

When he left, I sat there for a moment, trying to make sense of what had just happened. I didn't even know where to start. In tears, I drove straight to Lupe's house. I didn't want my mom or my sister to see me that way; all I knew was that a man had just rejected me and I needed a man to make me feel loved. I needed to hold on to Lupe's finger.

As I was driving, my cell phone rang. It was Chief. My heart jumped, thinking that maybe he had changed his mind. Maybe there was still hope. *Stupid Rosie.*

"I have one more thing for you to tell Lupe," he said.

"Okay, does this mean that you want to come with me?" I asked, excited.

"No. Just tell him that I don't love you."

My heart sank. He had just confirmed everything I had been thinking for practically my whole life—that I was unlovable and no one would ever want to marry someone like me.

Lupe opened the door and as soon as he saw the look on my face, he hugged me tight.

"Rosa, what's wrong?" he asked.

With tears rolling down my cheeks, I told him, "I'm pregnant."

His voice didn't change and he showed absolutely no signs of shock or surprise. He just hugged me tighter and said, "That's really cool! My baby is having a baby!"

How could I not love this man?

Lupe obviously knew the situation was not the best, but he was going to give me all the support I needed. His warm hug made me feel loved and protected.

Then he asked, "What's up with Chief?"

Crying, I answered, "He doesn't want to be with me. He says he doesn't love me."

"That's fine," said Lupe. "Don't worry. I can be your baby's daddy and will treat him or her as my own."

"But what am I going to do?" I asked. "How am I going to tell Mom and Dad? After all that I've put them through . . . and now this?" I felt so ashamed.

"I'll tell you what, Rosa," said Lupe. "I'm actually going to call a family meeting for tonight, so the timing is perfect."

He told me that he and his wife decided to get a divorce. The entire family knew they had issues in their marriage—along with all of the U.S. and Mexico—but Lupe wanted to make sure everyone was on the same page with how we were going to handle the media. "We will tell them everything at once," said Lupe. "Everything is going to be fine." His confidence reassured me.

That evening we all got together at Lupe's house. Juan and Chay were there, and so were Pete and Gus. Once Lupe was done confirming his news, he turned to me and said, "Rosa also has something to tell you."

With all the courage I could muster and my eyes filled with tears, I looked at my father and said, "Dad, I'm pregnant."

I closed my eyes and braced myself for the worst, but all I could hear was the sound of my mother crying.

"I could tell," she said almost immediately. "You have been sleeping too much these days and you barely eat. I knew you were pregnant."

Mothers always know.

Dad piped up, "And what's the problem, *mi* baby? A baby is a wonderful blessing, *Hija*. Just tell me how your daddy can help you."

When I explained that the baby's father didn't want to be with me and I had no idea how I was going to get through this by myself, Chay spoke up.

"Look at me, Sister. All these years I've raised my babies on my own and I can tell you, yes, you can do it," she said and smiled. "In fact, we'll do it together. You may be a single mom, but you are not alone, Sister. We're going to get through it together." She gave me the biggest hug ever, and right then and there, I knew my baby and I would be all right. My big sister and family had my back.

Within seconds, everyone gathered around me and joined the hug, saying, "Don't cry, Rosie. Everything is going to be all right."

As I stood there surrounded by all those beautiful faces who were embracing me and caring for me, I felt overwhelmed by all that love concentrated in one place. My family had stuck by me in the hardest of times and throughout my most troubled years—the years where I would systematically push them away—but they never once stopped loving me. And that big beautiful hug reminded me of that.

As devastated as I was by Chief's rejection, I was more devastated by the fact that it confirmed everything I'd always felt with Trino— I wasn't a virgin anymore so no one was ever going to love me. No one was ever going to marry me, not even the father of my child.

The damage inside me was so deep that I thought I wouldn't be a good mother to my baby and that she would probably be better off if I died and she became an orphan. At least that way, my mother or someone else would raise her and she would have a much better chance of becoming a good person.

The only thing that kept me going was school. It's strange; while I felt completely lost at the prospect of becoming a mother, when it came to school, I was able to stay focused. As broken as I was on the inside, I became determined not to be another college dropout statistic. So I pushed myself extra hard.

During my last two semesters at UCI, I took an internship at a law firm and worked part-time at a department store, all that while taking twenty units at school, one of which was a big thesis class. It was so hard. I gained sixty pounds during my pregnancy— my ankles were swollen, my hands were swollen, and I felt like an alien in my own skin. I was so depressed that I stopped trying to make sense of what was happening to me. I just went through the motions, working my way through the pain, as usual, hoping it would all be over soon.

I will never forget that around me, there was only silence. My family was there, they were right by my side, but they had stopped trying to talk to me. I wouldn't let them in. I was going through a lot and they all had compassion. I could see it in their eyes, but we wouldn't really talk about it. I remember one day Lupe and my mother were talking in the living room while I was sitting in front of the computer working on something for school. Suddenly, I began to cry. I was tired and lonely. I was thinking of how my child hadn't even been born yet and already I failed her because I hadn't been able to give her a good family. Dad always said family was all we had and to me that meant it didn't matter what I could give her—so as long as she didn't have her father with her at home, she wouldn't be completely happy. The tears just started to pour down my face. I cried and cried, gazing at the computer screen, not even trying to hold back. Suddenly, Lupe walked into my room. He got on his knees right beside me and hugged me.

"I know it's hard," he said. "I know it's really, really hard." His hug gave me strength to keep pressing forward.

During my pregnancy, another situation unfolded that made things even worse. My parents, the cornerstone of our family, our pillars, were going through a divorce. Our mother had found out our father was having an affair. We later learned that he had cheated on her their entire marriage and my mother knew it, but this time was different because he had gotten his lover pregnant. My mother—who up until then had been the hardworking, faithful, submissive wife of Don Pedro Rivera—decided that enough was enough. She asked him to move out of the house but he refused; he wasn't going to leave his family. She wasn't going to kick him to the curb so she resigned herself to kicking him out of their bedroom, and for the next several months they lived under the same roof without speaking a word to each other.

You could cut the tension with a knife. My siblings and I were devastated. At first we tried to get them to sit down and talk, but my father refused to say a word. He has never been one to express his feelings, and he kept absolutely silent. We would ask him, "Dad, is this true?" but he never gave an answer. He just stayed silent.

"Dad, say something, please," Juan begged him. "Papa, please don't let this family fall apart. This is all we have, Dad. Please save it."

But Dad wouldn't say a word. He must have been devastated inside, but he decided not to show it.

We didn't expect him not to take care of the child—we knew perfectly well that my father would have never done that; it would have been wrong. Yet all we wanted was for him to acknowledge what he had done and leave the woman. All he had to do was say he was sorry and Mom would have taken him back. But his pride got the best of him and he refused. Our entire universe was crumbling.

I was the only one living at home at the time so when everyone went home, I was left living in the Civil War. I was struggling to keep afloat amid the challenges in my own life—being pregnant, breaking up with Chief, graduating from college—and this just added to my despair. It was as if the rug was being pulled from under my feet because for my entire life, my father had told us that no matter what happens, no matter what you are going through, you always have family. "Family always comes first" is a maxim he engraved in our hearts. Yet at this particular moment, he wasn't putting our family first. He was letting it fall to pieces and I couldn't understand why he was doing it. Because the truth of the matter was, Dad didn't choose the other woman over my mom. He chose her over us. I will always admire and respect my father, but my heart was broken and it affected our relationship. He hurt my mother and to me, as women, we love, admire, and respect our fathers based on how they treat our mothers. The split was now between the women of the family and my dad.

My brothers and sister and I tried hard not to take sides but eventually the problems between our parents started to split the family in two. Some of the boys were more on my dad's side while Chay and I stood firmly by our mom. We knew she wasn't just being dramatic; we knew that she was acting this way because she had endured a lifetime of sadness and humiliation. She had forgiven his affairs many times in the past but when he got another woman pregnant, that was where she drew the line.

In those months as my tummy got bigger and I started to feel new life kicking inside me, I couldn't help but ask myself: if family is everything and my family is falling apart at home, then what is left?

The problems with my parents had shaken up my world and my concept of family, yet I continued to feel like such a failure for not being able to provide my daughter with a father. I knew Chief was far from being my knight in shining armor, but I couldn't help wanting to give my baby a real dad. I'd text him every day, hoping I could make him change his mind, begging him to come back to me.

But his response was always the same: "Leave me alone."

My family gave me such unbelievable love and support that I knew I could very well do without him, but I still hoped that we could have that happy family we had dreamed about when we first met.

During the nine months of my pregnancy, no matter how many times I begged him, Chief never came with me to a single doctor's appointment; he never even made the effort to call me and see how I was doing. What infuriated me the most was that he had started dating someone else. How could the father of my child be with another woman? How could he not care about his daughter? I simply couldn't wrap my head around it.

And then, my beautiful Kassey came into the world.

It was a Friday evening after my last day of classes at UCI and I started to have a high fever and back pain. I didn't know what was going on but as soon as I called the doctor, he told me to get myself to the hospital right away—he was worried it might be something serious so I drove myself there with my mom praying in the passenger seat.

When we got to the hospital, I found out the pain was due to a kidney infection. We didn't know the cause, but the doctors admitted me right away for an emergency induction because the infection was dangerous for the baby. I was so worried, and I didn't want to be all alone with my poor worried mother facing this ordeal so I immediately texted my best friend Gladyz, asking her to come join me, but also so she would let Chief and the rest of the family know what was going on.

Soon enough, they all started to trickle in. I was in labor for thirty-five hours, over the course of which I was accompanied first by Chiquis (who passed out) and my mom (who had to stay in the corner of the room because she couldn't stand the sight of blood). So in the end it was just me and my baby pushing through—a sign of what was to come over the following eight years.

On March 17, 2003, at five twenty p.m., the doctor handed me the most beautiful little girl I had ever seen in my life: Kassandra or Kassey, which is what we call her. Someone told me that in Greek mythology Kassandra was the name of a prophet and I replied, "Well, she certainly is the prophet of my life. Everything is going to be based around her now—she will guide me from here on out."

My brothers, their spouses, and my older nieces and nephews were all there and that March seventeenth quickly turned into a Rivera family celebration. Lupe was handing out the "It's a Girl!"

lollipops; Chay was trying to find a way to get all fifteen visitors in the room; Gus kept telling everyone how the baby looked just like him (he says that about all babies in the family and none of them look like him), Juan was entertaining the lobby guests, and Pete was praying and saying how proud he was of me.

At one point I was alone with my baby and was too shocked to cry until I heard our song, the song I had sung to my baby a hundred times on our commute to UCI while she was in my tummy: "Can't Take My Eyes Off of You"—a cover by Lauryn Hill. I decided right then and there that I would never give up on her, regardless of whether or not we ever had a man in our home.

When I brought Kassey home to my parents' house, the entire family was bubbling with excitement. A new baby is always a blessing, but this baby, my beautiful Kassey, was nothing short of a miracle because after months of not speaking to each other, my parents exchanged their first words. As the two proud grandparents fawned over her pretty little face and her tiny hands, my father said to my mother:

"*Ay, mira qué bonita está la niña, verdad, vieja?* Isn't she beautiful?"

"*Sí,*" she answered.

And that was the conversation starter. They never slept in the same bed again, they never had a relationship again, but at least they weren't enemies anymore. And that was a huge gain for all of us.

About two hours after Kassey was born, Chief showed up to meet his daughter—his spitting image. He came by after visiting hours since he wanted to make sure he didn't run into my brothers. The instant he held Kassey in his hands, he broke down and began to cry. Like me, he fell totally in love with her.

Amid the exhaustion and confusion of those first few days with Kassey, in the back of my mind I began thinking, *What if this precious baby turns him around? He clearly adores her—maybe he'll start loving me too?*

But of course I was wrong. During the pregnancy, I had gained sixty pounds and after Kassey was born, I weighed two hundred and sixty. Chief wanted nothing to do with me but he came around every weekend to see his precious little daughter.

My sister had taught me that unless it was an extreme situation (as was the case of Trino), you never keep your kids away from their father because it hurts the children more than it hurts him. So I decided to make the best of it. After Kassey was born, I started going on one crazy diet after another, thinking that if I managed to lose enough weight, Chief would have no other option than to fall back in love with me. I did everything I could to make myself attractive to him. I worked out four hours a day and went on an extreme diet but only lost twenty pounds; not enough to win him back. I went to a plastic surgeon and had liposuction to remove fat deposits from my stomach and hips. I would stop eating for days, and took diet pills that made me sick, but I didn't care. I just wanted to be thin. In my mind, being thin was synonymous with being loved so I was willing to do whatever it took.

I managed to lose some weight but in my mind it was never enough and I complained about it to my sister all the time.

Finally, one day Chay said to me: "You've got to stop throwing a pity party for yourself, Samalia"—one of the thousands of nicknames Chay had for me. "Do you really want to do something about your weight?"

"I do, Sister, I do!"

"Well, then," she said. "You need to imagine yourself the way you want to look and take the steps to get there. What do you think will help?"

In my frantic search for the magical solution to my woes, I had been reading about gastric bypass so I started telling Chay about it. But she immediately responded by saying, "I hear people have died from that."

"I'm going to die anyway," I answered, "so I might as well die thin. Bury me in a two piece if I'm skinny."

Chay convinced my parents to pay for the procedure and after that I lost about sixty pounds. But I still wasn't happy with myself.

What did give me a thrill, however, was a letter I received in the mail. I had applied to Whittier Law School in Costa Mesa, California, and jumped for joy when I was admitted. "I did it!" I shouted.

I was the first woman in our family ever to go to law school.

Amid all that turmoil, I managed to graduate from UCI with honors and a 4.0 average in my last two years. And I'd gotten into law school. That Christmas, Chay gave me the best present of my life. Chay was the best at giving presents. She always took the time to select the perfect gift for everyone in her life. That Christmas was particularly special though, because wrapped in a big gift bag with a large bow was a beautiful plaque that said:

FOREVER RESPECTED FOR YOUR
STRENGTH AND DETERMINATION.

I broke down crying when I saw it. The fact that the strongest woman I knew respected me meant the world to me. I've never loved myself, but when she gave me that plaque, I felt as if I had done something worthy of respect and admiration. I remember thinking, *I can love myself now. I have earned it.* Not because of the diploma but because I triumphed over everything that was supposed to break me, everything that was supposed to make me a statistic—I wasn't a high school dropout, I wasn't a college dropout, I was a single mom but even so, that didn't stop me. So that moment, when I was twenty-one years old, I finally started to love myself.

Or so I tried.

eight

a false start

In 2006, out of nowhere, one of my childhood friends popped back into my life. For years, Pedro had been close to our family and, with the exception of the abuse, knew everything about me—the good, the bad, and the ugly.

The first time I met Pedro was when we were about eleven years old. I met him through my brother Gus. He's the nephew of a friend of the family. For many years we were just acquaintances and we would meet at family parties and get-togethers. I didn't see him for many years, except, when I became pregnant with Kassey, he suddenly reappeared in my life. As soon as he found out I was expecting, he called me up to congratulate me. I thanked him and explained that I was happy but the circumstances weren't exactly great—I wasn't with the dad so as far as I could tell at the time, I was going to be a single mom. Pedro didn't seem to think that was a drawback. He was so happy for me and on the spot offered to help with anything I needed. All throughout the pregnancy he called and stayed in touch with me and slowly but surely, we became good friends. We talked a lot and no matter how hard things got for me, he always tried to make me smile and make me laugh. He was a very funny man, very hardworking, and in that sense he reminded me of the men in my family. At the time he was working hard at building his career as a car salesman and I really admired him for that. Eventually we became very close and I started to rely on him for support—he was a friend I could always talk to, but I still didn't see him as anything more.

He never disappointed me. He just kept showing up and showering me with attention. He called me every day just to see how I was doing. He was my shoulder to cry on, the person I shared anything good that happened in my life and no matter what I told him—whether it was that I was dropping out of law school or going out on a date with another guy—he supported me. "Don't worry, Rose, this is going to be good. You're going to be good."

After Kassey was born, he told me that he was in love with me. I thought he was nuts! Not only did I see him as just a friend, but also I was still overweight, I was a single mom, and my baby's dad didn't want to be with me. How in the world could he be in love with me?

But Pedro saw things differently. He admired me for being a single mom—in fact his mom had raised him on her own—and he wanted to take care of me. "Rosie," he'd say, "I am going to make you my queen and you'll never have to work another day unless you really want to." It obviously wasn't what I wanted, but the fact that he would say so made me feel like the most special person in the world. But I simply couldn't see him as anything other than a friend. I told him so, and asked him to stop declaring his love for me, so he did and we just continued to hang out as the best of friends. To me it was wonderful to know that I could count on his support and the fact that he cared so much about me and my daughter made me start to care more about myself. Whether I was looking for a lunch date, a gym date, or someone to go to the movies with, Pedro was always there.

Yet in my heart I was still stuck on the idea of getting back together with Chief. I wanted so badly for my little girl to have her father that for a long time, I continued to call him and text him, trying to convince him to be with me. He obviously didn't want me, but I felt that at least one day I'd be able to tell my Kassey how hard I really tried. I owed her at least that. My love for her was more than my pride, and even though I didn't love Chief anymore—I lost all respect for him when he started dating someone else while I was pregnant and sacrificing all I had for our child—I was still in love with the idea of him and me being Kassey's parents together.

I don't know if I would have ever stopped trying to get back together with him had it not been for Chief's mother, who over the course of our whole ordeal became a dear friend. One day while we were talking on the phone, she said something I will never forget: "Rosie, you are a wonderful girl, and I would love to have you as my daughter-in-law, but I don't want you to wait for him any longer. You need to get on with your life."

The fact that she was the one saying it to me finally made it click. My heart broke in a million pieces, but she was right: Chief didn't love me and there was no amount of convincing that was going to change his mind. So I gave up.

And who did I turn to?

Pedro, of course.

Here was a man who didn't judge me for my past, promised to make me happy, and wanted to take care me and of my baby girl. He absolutely adored Kassey and that for me was huge—almost more important than the fact that he loved me. I wasn't physically attracted to him, but I knew he was a good man and my daughter needed a man at home, not only on the weekends, which is when Chief saw her. So I said to myself, why not? But from the first day we started dating, I was completely honest with him. I told him that I was willing to give it a try, but I didn't love him.

"That's fine," he said. "You'll grow to love me. Just give me a chance."

It was late afternoon and Pedro and I were sitting in his car, drinking cheap wine, listening to Norah Jones and making out. We had been dating for about a month and despite the fact that I wasn't yet in love with him, things were going smoothly and I was happy.

Suddenly, between kissing, Pedro said to me, "Wouldn't it be great if you married me?"

"Yeah, baby, yeah," I responded. In the heat of the moment, I didn't really register what he was saying.

"I mean, seriously," he continued, all out of breath. "Would you marry me?"

I suddenly stopped and looked him in the eyes.

"Wait, what? Are you serious?" I asked.

"Yes, Rose, I'll make you my queen."

I knew he treated his mom and sister like queens and as far as I could tell, he was doing the same thing with me. I knew I didn't really love him, but did that really matter anymore? I'd tried so hard to find love; what if I just needed to let it find me? Ultimately, what mattered most to me at that point was that there was someone in the world willing to marry me, and I didn't want to let the opportunity pass. Pedro was a good man, his feelings were real, and that was good enough for me.

"Okay," I responded. "But we have to do it now."

"Okay!" he said, excitedly.

I immediately texted my girlfriend Danna and asked her to find me a wedding chapel where we could get married right away—I wanted to make sure we sealed the deal before he changed his mind. My friend, of course, thought I was crazy but knew I couldn't be deterred once I set my mind to something.

"I'm on it," she responded, and within the next ten minutes she called back with the information: we could get married at the Guadalupe Wedding Chapel in downtown L.A. There was someone there who could officiate the ceremony and handle all the paperwork.

Two minutes later we were on our way.

By the time we pulled into the parking lot, about thirty minutes later, I started to get cold feet. What was I doing? Was this really the way it was supposed to happen? This was my wedding day, darn it. Why wasn't I happy? I wanted so badly to believe that this was going to be my happily-ever-after, but something in the bottom of my heart was telling me it wasn't. I could feel it in my gut. I asked Pedro to give me a moment and I sat there in the car, thinking for about ten minutes . . . and I remember thinking ten minutes was a long time! Of course ten minutes are nothing when it comes to making such a big life decision, but I was desperate and when you're desperate you make stupid, rash decisions that will affect the rest of your life.

I told Pedro what I was feeling and right away he hugged me reassuringly and said, "Don't worry, Rose, this is going to be the beginning of our fantastic life together."

I looked into his big brown eyes. He seemed so happy and sincere that right then and there I decided to believe him. I needed to believe him.

With that, we walked into the chapel and there, before a justice of the peace and not a single friend or family member in sight, we exchanged our vows, pledged our love, and became husband and wife.

After the ceremony, Pedro and I drove back home to my mother's house to pick up Kassey, but I didn't tell a soul what I had done. I only whispered into Kassey's ear, "You're going to have a stepdaddy, and Mommy won't be alone anymore." Of course, she was too young to know what I was talking about, but I wanted her to know that we were going to be all right. It was our little secret. Pedro was going to love her like a father and at last she would be able to have the happy, perfect childhood I'd always dreamed of for her.

Yet as happy as I was for having found Kassey a dad, I started to freak out in regard to my family. They weren't going to like the fact that I eloped; they weren't going to like it one bit. *This isn't the way we do things,* I thought. *They're going to be hurt that I didn't even include them.* When I explained it to Pedro, he understood my concern and he was willing to do whatever it took for me to be happy. So I came up with a plan.

"Here's what we're going to do," I told him. "We're going to do this in reverse. First, you're going to propose to me, however you want to do it, and you'll meet with my father and ask for my hand in marriage." I figured that after Dad said yes, we could plan a proper wedding, a big reception, and no one would have to find out we had already been married. It was the perfect plan!

But of course, it didn't go as expected. Pedro wanted to propose to me in front of my whole family so we got our friend Hector to come and record the big event. But as soon as Pedro opened his mouth I had to ask him to stop the camera. My mom was so upset and she started telling us we weren't ready—she didn't think we should be dating, much less planning to get married. Lupe had tears in his eyes and he said to Pedro, "I have seen her suffer so much, I just want her to be happy. All I ask is that you don't hurt her." No one else really said anything but it was clear that they didn't approve of the engagement. Chay, especially, was very quiet. She knew I was making a mistake but she was going to stay by my side and make it with me. I didn't know what to think because if they didn't agree with the engagement they would have been horrified to learn we were already married.

In the end, my father gave us his blessing and we announced our plans to get married. Those were the best of days—and Pedro really did treat me like a queen. He would open every door for me, pay for every single one of my needs, shower me with gifts and compliments, and he even went as far as introducing me to everyone as his queen. My initial doubts about this marriage started to dissipate and I felt incredibly lucky to have found such a good man.

Three days later, however, the throne I thought I was sitting on began to crumble. We were at a restaurant, and I was dressed in one of my usual short skirts—clothes he admired and had seen me in so many times.

A few men near the bar began making comments. I didn't pay them much attention but Pedro interpreted their comments as flirting, and I could see the anger rising in his eyes.

"You better get some new clothes or you will wear mine," he said sternly. "I don't want you to wear those short skirts anymore."

I kind of dismissed his comment, thinking it was a spur-of-the-moment thing, but as days passed, he became more and more obsessive. He told me to stop smoking and drinking; he'd throw away my skirts, ask me not to wear makeup. Soon I wasn't even allowed to hang out with my sister! I didn't understand what was happening. This loving guy who had boosted my ego and lifted my spirits was suddenly changing on me. Everything he had loved and celebrated about me suddenly became a threat to him and I started to feel as if I was under constant surveillance. He wanted to control every single aspect of my life. It was as if he resented the fact that he had worked so hard to get me, and once he did, he was determined to keep me on a short leash.

I couldn't believe what he was asking of me. But I was so exhausted and so tired of all the drama that for the most part, I followed along. My problem was that even though to the outside world Pedro was just my fiancé, he was already my husband and no matter how irrational things seemed to me, there was one thing I knew for sure and it was that I didn't want to fail at my marriage.

His possessiveness continued to escalate and it got to a point where I was allowed to be only at school, at home, or with him. Anything else was strictly prohibited. And boy, did it get worse. One day he said to me, "I don't want you to brush your hair anymore," and when I dared to ask why, I was told that it was because he wanted me to look unkempt and ugly so I wouldn't be attractive to any man.

It's easy to think that a man is possessive and jealous because he loves you so much when in fact it's the opposite—he's seeing you only as a possession and not an independent person with her own life. The truth is, fear is the opposite of love and while Pedro thought he loved me, he was just afraid to be alone.

I did everything in my power to show him he could trust me, but nothing I said or did made him feel secure. What was most disconcerting was that each day started with, "You are the most amazing woman I have ever met," but by nightfall, I had turned into the most despicable woman on the planet. That is, unless it happened to be a night when he wanted to have sex with me, in which case he'd pour on the charm.

I was completely lost. Yes, he professed his love for me, and I believed him, but at the same time when in a fit of jealousy, he called me a whore, I believed him too. If my sense of self-worth was already shaky to begin with, Pedro's Dr. Jekyll and Mr. Hyde routine was managing to destroy the little self-esteem I had left. In so many ways Pedro's behavior confirmed everything I had ever suspected about men yet I didn't have the willpower to leave.

I remember one incident that took place just a few weeks into our secret marriage. We were spending the night together at a hotel and Pedro had been drinking. I was doing my best to stay out of his way by burying myself in my books but soon enough he started touching me and kissing me, wanting us to have sex. His breath was heavy with the smell of alcohol and he was a complete mess. I didn't want to sleep with someone who made me feel like trash.

As gently as possible, I pushed him away and said, "No, Pedro. Not tonight."

That wasn't what he wanted to hear, of course, so he quickly grabbed me by the arm, pinned me to the bed and forced me to have sex with him even though I was crying and begging him to stop hurting me. As soon as he finished, he opened the door and literally threw me out of the room.

There I was, standing in the hallway with barely any clothes on. I was so ashamed. How could it be that I was married to someone who was capable of doing something like this to me? I felt absolutely worthless. Here I was, reliving my past, but this time with a man who was supposed to love and cherish me.

I immediately started banging on the door, begging him to let me back in. But he refused to open it.

"Pedro, I beg you, please! Open the door!" I screamed. "Someone is going to see me, please let me in!"

I banged on the door for a while but since he still wouldn't answer, I had the brilliant idea of going down to the front desk for help.

"My husband is in room two thirty-two," I said to the night clerk. "I lost my key and now I'm locked out. Would you mind letting me in?"

The man stood there staring at me for a minute or so, and then said: "Your type isn't allowed here."

"Excuse me?" I replied, thinking there had to be a misunderstanding.

"Prostitutes aren't allowed here," he continued. "Please go away—if not I'll have to call the cops."

Humiliated beyond words, I thought, *Is this what it has come to? I'm being mistaken for a prostitute?*

I ran back to the room as fast as I could and started banging on the door.

"Please let me in!" I shouted. "Please, Pedro, let me in!"

Eventually Pedro was kind enough to get up off his butt and unlock the door. Still furious from what had happened before, he tossed the car keys at me and demanded: "Get out of here, you filthy whore. Just leave. I want nothing to do with you." He threw my clothes at me and told me to go home.

The next morning, the phone rang. It was Pedro, and he couldn't remember a thing from the night before. When I tried to refresh his memory, he began pleading and asking for forgiveness, promising me the world.

"Please, baby, please don't leave me," he begged. "I love you so much, Rose, I promise you I'll never hurt you again."

So, like a fool, I drove over to the hotel and picked him up. I prided myself on being an intelligent woman who had made it into law school, but I was falling into a "break up to make up" cycle without even realizing it. Every single time he mistreated me, the next day he would beg and promise he would never do it again, but then he would. The next time we got together, the ugly scene inevitably repeated itself and he became more and more violent toward me.

After three months of this emotional roller coaster, I began to drop a lot of weight. I wasn't wearing makeup, and my mother, always in tune with her sixth sense, said to me: "Rosie, this isn't you. A woman who is engaged is supposed to be completely happy and wanting to look her best. Here you are, planning your wedding, and you look like you'd rather die."

"Mom, don't worry, I really am happy," I'd say. "I'm just tired from all the work at school."

But my mother knew better than to believe me. She looked into my eyes and said: "*Hija*, listen to me when I tell you this: Pedro is not the one. And that's okay. I am praying for you to break up with him."

Her words reminded me of earlier days for I already knew my mother had clairvoyant powers. Whenever a boyfriend broke up with me, and I'd run to Mom and complain, "You were praying for us to break up, weren't you?" And she always admitted that she was.

But this time I told her, "Sorry, Mom, this is the one—no matter how hard you pray."

"*Hija*, there is something wrong here, and I can't put my finger on it. But I am telling you, it's best if you just call this whole thing off."

As hard as I tried to block my mother's words from my mind, I had to admit that she was right. I wasn't the same person anymore. I was attending classes, but I was far from being the warrior I had once been when I was in my senior year of college. I was working on getting a law degree because I supposedly wanted to be a lawyer, but my heart wasn't in it. I was so far removed from myself that I wasn't even being a good mother to my daughter. My mother took care of her most of the time, thank God, because I was barely able to keep it together myself. I was a shadow of my former self, but for whatever strange reason, I couldn't bring myself to make a clean cut.

It wasn't long before I went to the dean's office and told him, "I can't continue with my studies." I used the excuse "I'm a single mom and my daughter cries because I am gone so much." It was true, Kassey was miserable without me. But the thing I didn't share with the dean was that I had been interviewing attorneys and judges for one of my classes and had noticed that most were divorced, separated, or had a bed in their back offices because they were too busy to go home to sleep some nights. My daughter saw her father only on the weekends and if I became an attorney, her mom would be gone for at least eighty hours a week. I was confused about so many things, but I was certain that I couldn't do that to her.

I'm sure it wasn't the first time he had heard those words, because he seemed to genuinely understand. "I fully appreciate what you are going through," he responded graciously.

And just like that, all my dreams, all my hopes for the future were flushed down the toilet. I dropped out.

Not too long after my meeting with the dean, Pedro's mother took me aside one day and told me, "I love my son, but I don't think he treats you right, Rosie. I know my boy, and can see that he is possessive and jealous. He hurts you and is killing your spirit and your soul." She added, "I've known you since you were a little girl and I love you like a daughter, and I can't let him destroy you. I know he'll hate me if he ever finds out what I'm saying to you, but I can't stay quiet any longer. For your own good, Rosie, please, please get away from him. If you don't, I really fear for what might happen."

Whoa! I couldn't believe what she was saying. Even though I was capable of recognizing that Pedro's behavior was in no way normal, I guess part of me thought he acted that way because of me. I thought there had to be something intrinsically wrong with me because I always ended up with men like that. But hearing his own mother speak of him that way, I realized maybe it wasn't me.

Still, I was incapable of leaving. At age twenty-five I had already had an abortion, become a single mom, and dropped out of law school. I didn't want to add "divorce" to my long list of mistakes.

I remember thinking, *What is wrong with me? Can I get nothing right?*

Life was just too grim and all I wanted was for the pain to stop.

n i n e

i lift my hands

Lying on the street with my head on the curb, half naked and drunk tired from walking and asking God to kill me, I thought I would never wake up on this planet again. But then, I heard a voice coming from deep down inside me. It wasn't a voice I could actually hear; it was more of a vibration or a presence, and I can't explain it other than by saying that my soul heard it.

"That's enough," the voice said. "Go home!"

Immediately, I opened my eyes and looked around me. I had no idea how much time had passed but I was lying in the street at the exact same spot. And I was alone.

As I sat up, I heard the voice again. It was firm, but not angry: "That's enough," it said. "Go home!"

My mind flashed back to that morning, many years earlier, when a visiting speaker at our church had called me out and said God told him there had been an attack against my life. As far as I could remember, that was the last time I had heard from Heaven. I said to myself, *Rosie, ever since the abuse eighteen years ago, you have tried everything in this world to be happy. Has any of it worked? Do you feel any better now than you felt back then?*

The sun wasn't even up yet and I was half-naked, sitting in the middle of the street, completely alone. The answer was pretty obvious.

Then suddenly I thought: *could Mom have been right all along? She has never stopped telling me that God loves me—I've just never made the effort to really listen to what she is saying. What if He really could fill this gaping void inside me?*

Sitting on that pavement, my life had sunk to its lowest point. I was expecting to die yet instead, I had clearly heard the words, "Go home!" So I looked up into the dark sky.

"Where is my home?" I asked. I didn't want my home to be going back to Pedro, who raped and hurt me. I didn't want my home to be back with my mom—I didn't want to continue to make her suffer. Where was I supposed to go?

In the darkness, the Holy Spirit reminded me of what my mother had been telling me for all those years: "Jesus has His arms wide open—the way He was on the cross." That meant God loved me and He would receive me no matter what I had done.

Suddenly everything became crystal clear: my home wasn't with Pedro or with my mother. It was the church—that church whose door was always open. I had spent so many years looking for a way to heal and the church was the only place I hadn't looked yet.

I stood up, took a deep breath, and said to myself, *What do I have to lose?* So instead of continuing to walk toward South Central L.A., I turned around and started in a new direction. I spoke to God and said to Him, "I am tired. My feet hurt. Can You please help me find a ride? I promise I will go home and tomorrow I will come to Your church."

The sun was starting to come up and no more than twenty

seconds after I uttered those words, a car honked at me, pulled up to the curb, and out of the passenger-side window, a young man asked me, "Hey, do you need a ride?"

In the car were two African-American guys. As friendly as they seemed, this went against everything my mother had ever told me. *Don't hitchhike*, Hija, *and never get in a car with strangers,* she'd always say. That day, however, I had the feeling that somehow everything was going to be all right.

"I do," I answered.

"Where do you want to go?" the man asked politely.

I figured it was best to go back to my brother Lupe's house, which was the closest from where I was, so I said, "Would it be possible for you to drop me off on the corner of Lincoln and Manchester?" I didn't want to give them my brother's exact address in case it turned out they weren't such good guys.

"No problem!" said the driver, so I hopped into the backseat.

"You look cold," one of them said and turned on the car heater. And for the rest of the ride, they didn't say anything else.

Riding in the backseat, I was astonished. Tears welled up in my eyes as I thought, *Didn't I just ask God for something and He answered? He must have been paying attention all along.*

The two young men dropped me off at the corner of Lincoln and Manchester and as I made my way toward my brother's house, I couldn't stop asking myself, *Did this really just happen?*

To this day, I am convinced that those men that picked me up that night were angels.

Moments later, another car pulled up alongside me and I started to walk as fast as I could. The guys that had just given me a ride had turned out to be angels, but I doubted I could be so lucky twice.

"Rosie! Rosie!" I heard a voice shout out from behind me. "We've been looking for you like crazy!"

The fact that they knew my name reassured me.

"Who are you?" I asked as I turned around to make eye contact.

"We're friends of your brother Juan. We've been out here looking for you for hours."

Juan had tried calling me after he finished performing that night, but when I didn't answer, he started dialing all my friends. No one knew where I was, except a girl who remembered that I had gone over to Lupe's house.

A few hours went by and since my brother still hadn't heard from me, he started to get more and more worried. He got a bunch of his friends to drive around the neighborhood with him and, sure enough, they found some of the clothing I had discarded. They even found my cell phone on the street near a steep hill.

Juan, who is a big, muscular guy about six-feet-three and two hundred eighty pounds, climbed down that hill searching through the rocks, afraid of what he might find. His buddies called him with the news that they had found me and Juan came to meet us as quickly as he could. When he saw me standing outside Lupe's house, he broke down in tears.

"I thought we had lost you!" he said.

Seeing my big brother cry came as such a surprise. Could it be that he was actually crying for *me*?

"Don't ever do this to me again, Bubba. You're my baby sister and I love you. I have no idea what this guy Pedro has been telling you—or what he has been doing to you—but forget it, and forget him. He doesn't love you. But I do!"

I knew it was my brother speaking, but I thought, *Is God hear-*

ing this? Somebody loves me, and he even sent out a search team to rescue me.

I was in such a daze that Juan had to tap me on my cheek to get my attention.

"Listen, Bubba," he said, "you're going to be just fine. We're gonna get you some help. Just tell me what you need—I know you called us and we were all busy, but I promise it won't happen again. What do you need? What do you want to do? Tell me—anything."

What I said next must have come as a huge shock to him; in fact I could hardly believe I was saying it myself:

"There is one thing I'd like to do," I answered. "I'd like to go to church today."

My big brother was in tears. He himself had stopped going to church after the scandal with the person in our congregation, but he knew me well enough to be moved by my request.

"You bet, Sister. I'll get you there no matter what."

I slept at Lupe's house for a couple of hours, and when I woke up, I picked up the phone and called my mother.

"Mom, this is Rosie. What time is church today?"

I could almost hear her surprise on the other side of the line.

"Why?" she asked.

"Because I want to go with you. In fact, I'll come over and pick you up."

There was a long pause—and I could only imagine what was going through her mind. For years, I had been so reticent whenever she suggested I attend church. Now not only was I going—I wanted to pick her up. "Don't play games with me," she said. "If you're going to be my ride, you better show up because I can't miss church. So if you change your mind at the last minute, you still have to take me."

"I'll be there, Mom," I answered.

She was attending Primer Amor Church in Whittier, where my brother Pete is still the pastor.

It was the first Sunday in November 2005, and I have to say I didn't look my best—especially after surviving one of the worst nights of my life. My clothes were a mess, my hair needed brushing, and my head was throbbing with a massive hangover.

Mom was half-expecting me to have changed my mind when I drove up.

"Wow! You are really coming," she exclaimed, with a big smile on her face.

"Yes, *Mami*," I said quietly. I was quite nervous about having to face God after having run from Him for so long. I wasn't sure He cared, but for the first time in my life I was ready to pull back the curtain and let Him see everything that was inside of me. I wanted Him to see me for exactly who I was.

I walked through the doors of the church a nervous wreck, thinking, *These people are going to take one look at me and instantly assume that I am a good-for-nothing tramp.* That was clearly what I thought of myself and I assumed it's what everyone else saw. However, the moment I stepped inside the church, an unexpected sensation washed over me. I suddenly felt, *This is where I should have been my whole life. I'm finally home.*

To my delight, I had never felt so welcomed and loved. All my fears and worries seemed to melt away and I was invaded by a sense of peace. I took a seat in the second row with Mom as the service commenced. Onto the platform walked a group of singers that they called "the worship team." It was led by my nephew Petey, Pete's son, who was nineteen at the time.

I had watched him grow up from the sidelines and I'd always thought he was a shy boy. But not on that platform. With beautiful sincerity and authority, he led the singers and the congregation in "Levanto Mis Manos" ("I Lift My Hands").

The moment they began singing, I had the feeling that a spring of water had opened inside of me—as if a rock had been removed from a deep well and the water would not stop flowing. It was a release like I had never felt before. I couldn't control my tears as I listened to the powerful words of that song:

> *I lift up my hands,*
> *Even when I don't have strength*
> *I lift my hands*
> *Even with a sea of problems*
> *When I lift my hands . . .*
> *I can feel you love me.*

I had never heard the song before but I knew, from the bottom of my heart, that those words were true. I had lived my entire life fearing that God wouldn't love me if He saw the real me. But at that moment, everything changed. I finally understood what my mother had been telling me all along: God already knew everything about me and He loved me anyway. He still does.

Mom could see I was filled with emotion, but she gracefully refrained from making a big deal of it, allowing me to have my moment with God. But I could see from the corner of my eye that she, too, was crying.

I can't tell you what text my brother preached that day. At first I said to myself, *Maybe this is for others who haven't done the awful things I've done,* but then quickly I realized it was also for me.

When the message was over and Pete invited everyone in the congregation to come forward to pray, I knew this was my chance. But I was terrified. As I stepped into the aisle I knew perfectly well that this was what I had to do, but I felt as if I was dead inside. I was walking, but it felt as though I was dragging myself from being beat up in battle. Every step seemed like an eternity.

As I got closer and closer to the altar, the worship team started singing "I Lift My Hands" again and once more I felt that beautiful feeling of peace wash over me. Could I possibly be worthy of worshiping the Lord?

Suddenly, both of my hands were up in the air. Part of me kept feeling unworthy so I asked God, "Do You really know every nook and cranny of my life? Do You know that I killed my baby? Please forgive me, Lord." And as the beautiful music surrounded me in a warm embrace, I began relating my past sins, asking for forgiveness.

As I poured out my heart, a man I'd never seen before knelt beside me and said: "The Lord says, 'I love you.'" He prayed for me, then added, "Can I give you a hug?"

Through my tears, I replied, "Yes."

It was as if the Lord was there in person. The man kept repeating words from above. "I love you," he said. "I love you, I love you." I understood it was God speaking to me through this man so I drank up every word. Finally, after so many years of living out in the cold, I was finally letting down my guard and allowing God to love me.

No one can ever change my mind about what I felt at that moment. After so many years of going to church but not really being in church, I was finally starting to understand what it was all about. My Maker knew all my imperfections and all along I'd been mistaken. I didn't have to be perfect to be worthy of God. I just had to be me.

Then I heard a voice that came from Heaven itself: "Do you still want to take your life?" it said.

Immediately I answered, "Yes. It's hard to live with so much pain and sadness."

Next, the voice said, "What if we made a promise—a pact?"

"Okay," I answered.

He continued: "What if you die to your feelings and your emotions? What if you die to your hatred toward Trino? What if you die to your vengeance and bitterness? What if you die to everything Rosie has ever wanted, and you start to live for me?"

For a moment I mulled over the questions as I didn't want to make any empty promises. Then, I started to remember all the stories I had been told as a child. I saw Jesus dying on the cross— and now I knew it was for me. The King of Kings had a million angels at His command, and He could have sent one of them my way. Instead, He left His throne, came to Earth, and gave His life for Rosie. I understood what God was asking. So I prayed, "If You did this for me, I happily say 'yes' to dying to my past and current feelings. I say 'yes' to dying to my own plans and dreams. I promise I will never say 'no' to You again."

As I was talking with God, another individual came up to me—a lovely woman of about sixty years of age, with gray hair. She looked so wise and knowledgeable.

"May I pray with you?" she asked.

I said yes, of course, and she began to pray. The woman repeated exactly what the first gentleman had told me, "God says, 'I love you.'" And she kept saying, "I love you. I love you, I love you." Over and over again.

My heart continued to melt.

Suddenly, a third person was by my side, a woman in her forties. I could hardly believe it when she whispered, "God is saying, 'I love you.'"

I was in awe. *Could this be a coincidence? Had someone*

planned it? But then I remembered no one knew I was going to be there, not even me.

That day, I understood God's limitless power. His limitless love. Knowing that everything about my life was out of order, I told God, "I am ready to die to self and live for You, but I need Your help." And I pleaded, "I don't know if I should go back to my husband. I am terrified of him. Please help me."

Those moments at the front of the sanctuary, pouring my heart out, did more for me than anything I had ever found in all my years of running. I left church that day, breathing a deep sigh of relief, as if a ton of weight had been lifted from my shoulders. I felt loved and light in spirit, just like the princess my dad always said I was.

On the ride home I remember thinking, *What's come over me?* I didn't feel guilty about my past anymore. The pain that had weighed on my spirit for so long was lifting. Then I heard the little voice inside me say, "This is the peace I give you."

Mom was very quiet in the car, but at some point I felt the need to say something about what I had just experienced.

"I really enjoyed the service," I said, trying to keep it as simple as possible. "I felt something very beautiful."

She reached over and patted my cheek, smiling.

"I know, *Hija*, I know."

As soon as I found a minute alone, I called my sister, Chay, to tell her about what had happened.

"Rosie, I'm so sorry I didn't get to talk with you last night," she said as soon as she picked up the phone. "How are you?"

"I am so happy, Sister," I said.

"Why?" she asked, somewhat surprised. It really wasn't like me to say I was happy.

"Well, I went to church today and I can't put into words what happened, but did you know that God loves me?"

She kind of giggled. "Yes, He loves you, Sister."

"No, Sister, I mean He really, really loves me," I said. My voice cracked a little, I was getting emotional.

I could just see the smile on her face as she said, "Rosie, of course God loves you. You are very very lovable and we all adore you."

"Really?" I asked in disbelief.

"Yes, Sister," she continued. "You are the easiest person to love."

I paused for a moment, and then said to her, "Sister, I'll tell you what. I'm going to stop drinking."

"Oh, that's great," she said, a tinge of surprise in her voice.

"And I'm going to stop smoking, too," I continued.

"That's wonderful!" she said.

"From now on, I am going to live a different life."

I could tell she was surprised, but she was also excited. "I'm so proud of you," she said.

And that was when I dropped the bombshell: "And you know what, Sister? I'm not going to have sex anymore."

There was a long pause, after which finally she shot back, "Whaaat???"

"I am going to practice abstinence until I get married."

At that point, no one knew that Pedro and I had eloped as I still hadn't mustered the courage to tell the truth. But what I was really telling myself was that things had changed, and from that day forward, I was going to practice abstinence.

The thought of me quitting sex was so inconceivable that Chay couldn't help but burst into laughter. "I know you," she said, still giggling. "How will you be able to do that?"

"I'm not sure," I replied. "But I know God can help me."

Chay, who believed in a higher power even though she didn't regularly attend church, said, "I'm so proud of you, Sister. I know this is going to be great for you. Whatever you need, you know I'm here for you."

That afternoon, I told my mother, "I made some real decisions this morning. You're going to see a big change in me."

My mother was thrilled to hear me say that, but of course she had her doubts. Was all this just a passing whim? Or was I going to be able to sustain it? Was I serious about what I was saying or would it soon blow over? But as days turned into weeks and weeks turned into months, my mother and the rest of my family started to notice a drastic change in my disposition. Instead of sulking around and being constantly angry and unhappy, I would smile every day. Problems would pop up and I'd say, "Don't worry about it," without stressing or flipping out.

From the instant I stepped out of the church that fateful morning, there was no more alcohol in my life. To this day. From time to time, I would still go to parties with Chay and my friends, but never again did I drink or use drugs. At the beginning, it came as a surprise to the people who knew me, but soon enough they realized that I was serious about the change in my life and respected me for it. God breaks chains of addiction and those who have been healed have to make the effort to see those changes stay permanent.

As drastic as it was for me to stop drinking and smoking and having sex, what became the biggest shift in my life was that I wanted to be in church every time it opened its doors. It was my home, the place where God had said, "I love you," and I wanted to spend as much time in there as possible.

LEFT: Nine months old. I was my parents' unexpected surprise; love was all I knew. / IZQUIERDA: A los nueve meses de edad. Fui una sorpresa inesperada para mis papás. Amor, eso es lo único que conocía.

BELOW: First birthday and baptism. I was Lupe's spoiled baby sister from the moment I was born. / ABAJO: Mi primer cumpleaños y mi bautismo. Fui la bebé consentida de Lupe desde el momento en que nací.

All photos this page by Pedro C. Rivera

In the vulnerable days when I still gave my heart to animals.
My puppy Huevo was one of our many pets. / En mis primeros y frágiles años
cuando entregaba todo mi corazón a los animales. Mi perrito Huevo
era una de nuestras muchas mascotas.

Pedro C. Rivera

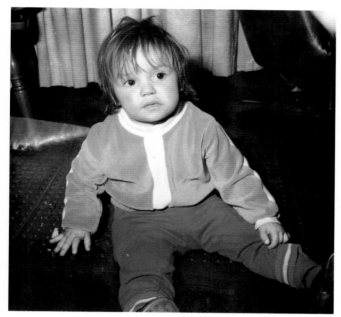

As a child I was so fair and blond, people would ask my dad if he was my babysitter! People are still surprised when they find out I speak Spanish. / Como era de piel muy clara y cabello rubio, ¡la gente le preguntaba a mi papá si él era mi niñero! Aún hoy en día le gente sorprende que hable español.

Juanelo and I always had a blast together. The coolest guy on the block happened to be my older brother and protector. To date, he is my closest male friend and still the coolest guy I know. / Juanelo y yo siempre la pasábamos muy bien. El niño más genial de la cuadra era nada más y nada menos que mi hermano y protector. Hasta la fecha, es mi amigo más cercano y el hombre más sensacional que conozco.

All photos this page by Pedro C. Rivera

ABOVE: Juanito, Trino's nephew, and me at a Quinceañera or wedding. Our families thought we'd be friends forever; sadly we didn't even exchange a hello many years later at the trial. / ARRIBA: Juanito, el sobrino de Trino, y yo en una fiesta de Quinceañera o en una boda. Nuestras familias pensaban que seríamos amigo para siempre. Tristemente, años después ni siquiera nos saludaríamos durante el juicio.

RIGHT: Playing hard with the boys resulted in a dirty but happy child. I allow my kids to have fun and get down and dirty like I did. / DERECHA: Jugaba mucho con los niños y por lo tanto fui siempre una niña siempre sucia, pero feliz. Yo permito que mis hijos se diviertan y se ensucien.

All photos this page by Pedro C. Rivera

Four years old.
Mami and I in
Monterrey, Mexico.
The strongest woman
on Earth. Warrior
on her knees. / A los
cuatro años de edad.
Mi mamá y yo en
Monterrey, México.
La mujer más fuerte
del mundo. Una
guerrera de oración
arrodillada.

Poverty was
overshadowed by
love and joy. / La
pobreza no era nada
comparada con el
amor y la alegría.

All photos this page by Pedro C. Rivera

Daddy was an aspiring photographer and took hundreds of pictures of us. Rosie the car model. / A mi papi le habría gustado ser fotógrafo profesional y tomó cientos de fotos de nosotros. Rosie, la modelo de autos.

My family gave me a wonderful childhood. I pray to give the same smiles, laughs and life lessons to my children. / Mi familia me dio una infancia maravillosa. Deseo dar a mis hijas las mismas sonrisas, risas y lecciones de vida.

All photos this page by Pedro C. Rivera

Seven years old. My mother dressed me like a traditional Mexican girl as long as she could. I thought I was a Mexican princess. / A los siete años de edad. Mi mamá me vistió con ropa tradicional de niña mexicana por tanto tiempo como pudo. Yo pensaba que era una princesa mexicana.

Pedro C. Rivera

Eight years old. Through the years, my pictures reveal the change in my demeanor and personality. My smile was not as wide, and I became shy and introverted after the abuse began. / A los ocho años de edad. Con el paso del tiempo, las fotos muestran el cambio en mi apariencia y personalidad. Mi sonrisa ya no era tan amplia y me volví tímida e introvertida después de que comenzó el abuso.

Melody and me at Garfield Elementary. One of my very few friends; sometimes it's still difficult for me to socialize. / Melody y yo en la escuela primaria Garfield. Una de mis pocas amigas. Aún me resulta difícil socializar.

All photos this page by Pedro C. Rivera

Nine years old. I began to dress more like a boy to avoid attention
from men. / A los nueve años de edad. Comencé a vestirme como niño para
evitar llamar la atención de los hombres.

Pedro C. Rivera

Chay and me. At thirteen years old, I was very overweight, but when people told me I looked like Chay, it was, and still is, the greatest compliment ever. She was the most beautiful woman I knew. / Chay y yo. A los trece yo sufría de un sobrepeso considerable, pero cuando la gente me decía que me parecía a Chay era —y aún es— el mayor cumplido que me podrían haber hecho. Ella era la mujer más hermosa que he conocido.

Pedro C. Rivera

Daddy and me. If I could only be his little girl forever. / Mi papi y yo. Desaría ser su niña chiquita por siempre.

Gustavo L. Rivera

Lupe and me. Wherever my brothers and sister performed, I was in the front row singing every song. A happy fan and proud sister. / Lupe y yo. No importaba dónde se presentaba mis hermanos, yo estaba en la primera fila cantando cada una de las melodías. Una fanática feliz y hermana orgullosa.

Eighteen years old. No matter what state my heart was in, I smiled for Daddy's camera. I yearned to make him proud. / A los dieciocho años de edad. Sin importar cómo estuviera mi corazón, siempre tenía una sonrisa para la cámara de mi papi. Deseaba hacerlo feliz.

All photos this page by Pedro C. Rivera

Twenty-one years old. Mami, Nana Lola, Kassey and me after my college graduation. I graduated early, with honors and a three-month-old baby but still felt like a failure. / A los veintiún años de edad. Mi mami, mi nana Lola, Kassey y yo después de mi graduación de la universidad. Me gradué antes de tiempo, con honores y con un bebé de tres meses, pero aun así me sentía un fracaso.

Twenty-eight years old. Chay and me at our birthday party on a yacht. After I ruined her twelfth birthday party, neither of us ever celebrated alone again. / A los veintiocho años de edad. Chay y yo en nuestra fiesta de cumpleaños en un yate. Después de que arruiné su fiesta de cumpleaños número doce, ninguna de las dos volvimos a celebrarlo solas.

All photos this page by Pedro C. Rivera

Jacob Yebale, Mom, Chay and me getting ready for Chay's wedding ceremony.
I had never seen a smile as beautiful as hers that day. / Jacob Yebale, mi mamá,
Chay y yo preparándonos para su boda. Nunca había visto una sonrisa tan
hermosa como la que ella nos regaló ese día.

Mom, Chay and me. Chay always blessed me with incredible moments,
such as dressing her for her big day. Those moments are the prized possessions
of my heart. / Mi mamá, Chay y yo. Chay siempre me bendijo con momentos
maravillosos, como cuando la vestí para su gran día. Esos momentos son
lo más preciado de mi corazón.

ABOVE: Mom, Chay and me praying before she walked down the aisle. What an honor and a joy to be able to pray for my sister. / ARRIBA: Mi mamá, Chay y yo rezando antes de que Chay comenzara a caminar hacia el altar. Qué honor y felicidad poder rezar por mi hermana.

RIGHT: When Chay asked me to be her maid of honor, I was shocked because she has so many famous friends. She replied, "Who else could it be, Sister?!" / DERECHA: Cuando Chay me pidió que fuera su dama de honor me quedé sin palabras, porque ella tenía muchos amigos que eran famosos. Me respondió "¡¿Quién más podría serlo, hermana?!".

All photos this page courtesy of Jenni Rivera Estate–Hazelnut Photography

Once again on the dance floor, fifteen years after we had danced at my Quinceañera. We laughed, hugged and cried for joy. / De nuevo en la pista de baile, quince años después de que bailáramos en mi Quinceañera. Nos reímos, abrazamos y lloramos de felicidad.

Courtesy of Jenni Rivera Estate–Hazelnut Photography

July 4, 2011. Chay, Pastor Pete, Abel and me. She stood by my side as I searched like a madwoman for love, and celebrated with me with tears in her eyes as my matron of honor. / 4 de julio de 2011. Chay, el pastor Pete, Abel y yo. Ella permaneció a mi lado mientras yo buscaba enloquecidamente el amor, y celebró conmigo, con lágrimas en los ojos, cuando fue mi madrina de bodas.

Courtesy of the Flores-Rivera Family Trust–Tippol Photography

ABOVE: The day I was redeemed and loved beyond my wildest imagination . . . and the last day my whole family would all be together. / ARRIBA: El día en que fui redimida y amada como nunca podría haber imaginado . . . y el último día en que mi familia entera estaría reunida.

LEFT: Abel, Kassey and me. Where your heart is, there is your treasure. This is the treasure I searched for my whole life . . . and found, thanks to Christ. / IZQUIERDA: Abel, Kassey y yo. En donde esté tu corazón, encontrarás un tesoro. Este es el tesoro que busqué toda mi vida . . . y lo encontré gracias a Cristo.

All photos this page courtesy of the Flores-Rivera Family Trust–Tippol Photography

. . .

God gave me back my life but my biggest challenge during this time was deciding what to do about my husband, Pedro. We were still legally married, but we weren't yet living together and were still in the middle of planning our fake wedding.

Since I had vowed to abstain from having sex until we were properly married, I used every excuse in the book not to be with him. He was, needless to say, very upset—not just because I refused to be intimate with him, but also because he was totally baffled by the huge change in my behavior. I wasn't so down and depressed all the time and in my dealings with him, I was becoming less and less submissive. I tried, many times, to get him to come to church with me but every single time he refused. For him, the only explanation for the change in my behavior was that I had to be having an affair with someone in church. He wasn't so far from the truth, since I had fallen in love with Jesus Christ.

For the following two months, Pedro would wait for me outside the church—accusing me of sleeping with someone in the congregation. He simply couldn't understand why I was there so often.

Over the course of those two months, it became so clear to me that we were not right for each other. In my brain, I finally knew what my heart had been trying to tell me: our marriage was never going to work. Pedro and I had been two emotionally unhealthy individuals, desperate for love, who had just happened to find each other at a vulnerable time in their lives. We shared a powerful sexual attraction and while we were enamored with the idea of being in love, the fact of the matter was that we weren't.

Day after day, I would ask God for help on how to deal with my predicament. Even though I was sure we weren't going to be able to be together, I still grappled with the issue of divorce. I was still hung up on the fact that I didn't want to add another item to my list of failures. So I prayed to God: "Please show me what path I need to take."

My reading habits took on a radical change too. Instead of wasting my time reading trashy novels and porn, I was now reading the Bible every spare moment I had. One day my eyes focused on these words by an Old Testament prophet: "I will give her . . . a door of hope; she shall sing there . . . 'And it shall be, in that day,' says the Lord, 'That you will call Me "My Husband"'" (Hosea 2:15–16).

I had walked into the door of my new home, been given a new song, and was united with God. Upon reading that verse, I knew now that the earthly marriage I had hastily entered into was not part of Heaven's plan for me. I was going to turn my life to God.

The next day, there was total peace in my heart when I asked Pedro for a divorce. His reaction was saying "No way!" believing that my turn toward spiritual matters was just a passing fad. But he was wrong.

Pedro continued to pursue me for several months, always calling me and waiting for me outside of church, begging for us to get back together. But I stayed firm. As time passed he started to come by less and less, mostly just to check up on Kassey, whom he was always so good to.

A year went by and then one day I got a call from Pedro telling me that he had met someone and he couldn't keep coming around to see me. I was happy for him but also sad because it made me realize that throughout the whole ordeal I had lost my friend.

I wanted us to get a divorce right away, but Pedro didn't want to. The person who saved me, once again, was Lupe. At the time I was working as a real estate agent and my brother wanted to buy a beautiful ranch up north and he wanted to put the house under my name in order to get the loan from the bank. There was just one problem: I was married! I couldn't let Lupe put the ranch under my name because that would mean it also belonged to Pedro. I explained the whole situation to Lupe (who was shocked, of course) and together we decided to ask Pedro to please sign the divorce papers, if not for me, for Lupe.

Pedro ultimately understood the situation and he finally accepted. He loved and respected Lupe and he wanted to make things right. A couple of weeks later we went to the courthouse and signed the divorce papers. It was remarkably anticlimactic, and I realized I had made that legal union out to be a bigger deal than it really was. I immediately told my family to forget about any future wedding plans; Pedro was no longer a part of my life.

Shortly thereafter, I stood before the congregation and shared my story. I said it all. For the first time in my life, I spoke of all my secrets and explained that my name in Greek means "secret" but that the truth would set me free. With my mom in the front row, I unveiled every single nook and cranny of my life, including my promiscuity and the fact that I had eloped with the first guy who asked. My family, who was in the audience, was blindsided by the news of my elopement, but I felt it was time to be totally honest with God and with them. They were shocked and surprised, but they breathed a sigh of relief that this particular episode of my life had finally come to an end.

ten

breaking free

The change came immediately. My transformation was dramatic and from the inside out. It was as if a dense fog had been cleared from my mind and I could finally see life's higher purpose. I wasn't just some sexually abused single mother, law school dropout, and divorcée. I was so much more. Those labels that for so long had weighed so heavily on my soul no longer mattered. I didn't care. Others may have thought I was useless, but I no longer saw myself that way.

Now I was happy, joyful—I was even singing in the choir. However, there were other issues whose roots were deeply seeded in my soul—including my anger toward Trino and the psychological aftermath from the years of abuse—and those would involve a longer and more complicated process. It was as if after such a huge revelation—the discovery that God really loved me—I was able to let go of all my exterior chains, but what was going on inside my head was an entirely different problem.

I sought counseling. It did not solve all of my problems, but the sessions certainly gave me the tools to take a long hard look at my life and make some changes. It was a long process that involved a great deal of trial and error, but ultimately I started to acquire the tools that would help me break with certain thoughts and behaviors while confronting the pain from my past experiences. I had gone to therapy many times before, but this time, for the first time, my heart was truly open to change.

I found an outstanding Christian counselor, who treated me as if I had Post Traumatic Stress Disorder (PTSD)—a disorder that usually affects people who have been to war or suffered through a deeply traumatic event. The truth was, ever since the tender age of eight, I had been waging an emotional war against myself. Now that I had found God's love, I was at last able to take a step back and look at my life for what it was; I was able to analyze my feelings, understand my behaviors, and ultimately let go of all the hatred and sadness that had weighed me down for so many years.

It was a time of so much self-reflection. I spent hours reading, writing, and thinking about my life, my family, my loves, my daughter. *Everything.* It wasn't always easy—change never is—but I felt powerful and loved, and for the first time in as long as I could remember, I was starting to feel as though I could take on the world. Deep down inside of me, a tiny voice was reminding me of what my father had said to me all those years earlier when I was a little girl: "You can be anything you want, *Hija.* Anything at all."

Knowing I was just taking baby steps down my new path, one day I asked my brother, Pastor Pete, how I could prepare myself for what the future might hold. Having lived through so many devastating events, part of me was still afraid of the future and I knew I needed to ground myself in order to move forward.

Pastor Pete encouraged me to enroll in Angelus Bible Institute, a multilingual Christian college on the campus of the renowned Angelus Temple in Los Angeles. Because of my speaking and preaching ability, Pastor immediately saw potential in me to become an evangelist. When he first mentioned it to me, I was shocked because I have always considered myself to be a shy person, afraid to look others in the eye. But now that I had found the Lord, I was suddenly filled with a desire to speak to anyone and everyone about His love.

The classes I took there were unlike any I had ever experienced. Yes, I had a four-year college degree and one year of law school under my belt, but I had never encountered truth like this. Being the big nerd that I am, I had always enjoyed going to school and learning new things, but at the Angelus Bible Institute, I experienced learning like I never had before. Everything I learned there wasn't only feeding my mind; it was feeding my soul. Many days, I would sit in a lecture filled with emotion, so grateful for what I was hearing. The fact that everything that we discussed in class had such a clear and potent repercussion in the real world and in my life made me connect to my topic of study like never before. I had enjoyed classes in law school, but the truth was that deep down inside I had done it all because I wanted to get back at Trino. The classes at Angelus, however, were for *me* and *me* alone. Every day I went there, I was filling my heart with God's love and it felt so good.

One morning, a professor read a verse from the Bible, Acts 1:8, that said, "But you will receive power when the Holy Spirit has come upon you, and you shall be witnesses to Me in Jerusalem, and in all Judea and Samaria, and to the ends of the earth."

I immediately thought, "That's me!"

I looked up the word "witness" and found that in the late fourteenth century, Christians used the word as a literal translation of the Greek word *martys* or "martyr." I couldn't believe what I was reading. Hadn't I made a pact with God, saying that I was willing to die to myself and live for Him?

I wasn't sure what Jerusalem meant in all this. Was I supposed to fly over to Israel to share my story? But of course that wasn't what the verse meant at all. The biggest mistake one can make when starting to read the Bible is to take it too literally, and that was exactly what I was doing.

So I asked God what he meant by "Jerusalem" and that was how I understood that I was to let go and die to the hatred of my past—and that "Jerusalem" in my case meant *home*. I was to be a witness here at home, starting with my own family, and those I love. Reaching Israel, the Middle East, and the rest of the world would come, but it was for another day. I had to start right here.

Once I understood that, I was still confused by "Samaria." If the line said I would first have to go through Samaria, what did that mean?

I did some research on Samaria and learned that in biblical times, the inhabitants of Samaria were such enemies of the Jews that Israelites would literally travel the long way around the territory of Samaria in order to reach their destination. I understood what God was telling me. He was saying that I had to be a witness to those I loved, but also to my enemies.

My thoughts immediately went to Trino. He had been my enemy since I was eight years old and after years of trying to avoid him, I needed to prepare to face him as well.

. . .

During this time, my attention was called to another story in the New Testament. The Book of Acts records the account of the first martyr of the Church.

His name was Stephen. The man was simply bearing testimony to—or *witnessing*—the Lord when he was brutally attacked by a group of men "who were unable to cope with the wisdom and the Spirit with which he was speaking."

What was amazing to me when I read this story was that Stephen didn't even try to defend himself. Never once did he say, "Stop! I'm the good guy here! Don't listen to them. I am totally innocent!"

Instead, filled with the Holy Spirit, Stephen looked up into the heavens and beheld God's glory. "Look," he said. "I see heaven open and the Son of Man standing at the right hand of God."

They accused him of blasphemy and ultimately dragged him out of the city and started stoning him. Undisturbed by their violence, Stephen prayed, "Lord Jesus, receive my spirit," and then he cried out, "Lord, do not charge them with this sin." In other words, he was asking God to forgive them. Then Stephen laid down his life.

When I read this, I tried to put myself in Stephen's place. Could I ever respond like that? The more I thought about it, the more I understood: Stephen was just as innocent as I was. He was targeted for no valid reason, but he stayed focused and did what God told him to do.

My problems had begun way back in my childhood. I had had plenty of time to think about them and rationalize them, yet I still couldn't forgive the pain and suffering that had been inflicted upon me. But thinking back at Stephen, he was asking God to forgive his attackers right then at that very moment. I asked myself, "Where did he learn such compassion?" Then I was reminded that

Stephen knew of what had taken place just a few months earlier, when Jesus, on the cross, cried out, "Father, forgive them, for they know not what they do."

Just like the Son of God, Stephen was feeling the pain being inflicted on his body—the accusations hurled at him, and the sting of bitter hatred. But this witness made a decision to follow Christ's example. The martyr's story so impacted me that I wanted to have the mercy of Jesus. I wanted to be like Stephen and in order to do so, I knew I had to do one thing: forgive Trino.

Although my mind now understood what I needed to do, my heart simply couldn't follow. How could I forgive the unforgivable? How could I forgive a man who had stripped me of my child-hood? Not only had he taken my virginity; he had robbed me of my youth and my dreams. He had destroyed the innocent little girl who, sitting on her daddy's lap, believed she would one day be an astronaut, a teacher, or a writer.

And now I was expected to *forgive* him?

All this time I had been thinking about the effect of Trino's actions on me but I'd never really stopped to think what was going through Trino's mind. Was he sick? Was he deliberately evil? Was he aware of the consequences that his actions would have on the rest of my life? Could he have possibly imagined the lasting pain he would inflict on me—the drugs, the sexual issues, my unhealthy relationships with men?

Then a thought flashed in my brain. "Well, Rosie, you didn't know the depth of your wrong when you had an abortion!"

That really hit home.

Practically my whole life, I had thought Trino had to have been abused when he was a child; *something* had to have happened to him for him to behave that way. I tried so hard to come up with every possible excuse for what he had done. I was trying to find a *reason*. But when I thought about my abortion, I realized my thought process was completely different. I was able to be much harder on myself: I knew I had plenty of excuses, but there was no reason. *Nothing* justified my actions, just like *nothing* justified his. I had to accept his behavior for what it was. I had to stop trying to explain it.

God was telling me, "Don't diminish his actions, Rosie. Don't try to explain them. Take sin for what it is, and forgive it. I want you to pardon everything he did, whether he knew it or not."

"But how can I possibly do that?" I asked God.

"Forgiveness is not an emotion," He said to me. "It's a decision." Then He added, "You can make that choice right now. And if you do, there are great benefits for you."

This was a huge revelation for me. I had always thought that if I forgave Trino, he would have the most to gain. His slate would be wiped clean and he'd never have to suffer the consequences. He would get off scot-free and there would be no justice.

I had also always thought that I had to *get* to a place where I could forgive him. I never thought I could simply decide to forgive. Yet soon it became quite clear to me that if I forgave Trino, like Stephen of old, the power of God's Spirit would fill me and I could be a witness and see Heaven's glory—which I wanted more than anything in this world.

Then I heard a voice say, "Did you notice that Jesus gave Stephen a standing ovation?" I opened my Bible and read the story again and, sure enough, upon arriving in Heaven, Stephen saw Jesus "standing" at the right hand of God. It was as if the Lord was saying, "When your brothers and sister sing at a concert, there is usually an encore. People clap, and shout, 'Bravo! Give me more.

I'm really proud of you.' Wouldn't it be wonderful if you heard that from Me?"

That's when I understood that there was no difference between being a martyr of the early days and a martyr of today. I wanted to feel what Stephen felt. I wanted to show God what I am capable of. And from the moment that day in church, when I decided to die to myself and forgive what I thought was unforgivable, God promised to do the rest.

I promised the Lord that I was willing to love and forgive to such an extent that when the moment comes that I am taken home, I will be able to lie before Him and, like Mary, wash His feet with my tears and dry them with my hair.

What God asked me to do next was something I would have never considered on my own. I was to take a pen and paper and write down every count I had against Trino—as if I was a prosecutor in a trial. Then He said, "I want you to turn the list over to Me and let Me be the Judge."

By doing this exercise a huge weight was lifted off my shoulders. I no longer needed to think about Trino. I no longer needed to decide whether what he had done was right or wrong. I didn't need to even think about it. God was going to take care of it.

So I began writing—1 . . . 2 . . . 3 . . . 5 . . . 10 . . . 20 . . . 30 . . . 40 counts, and the number kept increasing. When I reached 101 counts of physical, emotional, psychological, spiritual, relational damage he had caused, I turned the list over to God and told Him: "It's in Your hands."

"Look at the list again," He said. "Many of these counts are Trino's fault, but there are plenty of sins here that are the result of your own choices."

And he was right, of course. Trino had damaged me in so many ways, but after a certain point my decisions had been my own and I couldn't blame him for everything bad that ever crossed my existence. I needed to accept my part. And that made me ask myself: how could I ask God to forgive my sins if I wasn't capable of forgiving Trino for his?

It wasn't an easy realization, but it was a powerful one. I needed to forgive Trino in order to forgive myself. Once I understood that, I knew exactly what I needed to do but I couldn't wrap my mind around it. How was I going to change a feeling that had been so deeply ingrained in my heart for so many years? Hating Trino had become part of my identity and I wasn't sure I remembered what it even meant to be Rosie—just Rosie.

I understood what needed to happen, but in the most literal sense, I didn't know what to do. I felt that if I prayed, "Lord, please forgive Trino," I would be lying since I didn't really feel it in my heart. I struggled with this a great deal. I wasn't able to decide what to do. Until one day from deep down inside me, the realization came to me that if I had no other words, I should just say, "God bless Trino."

I learned that saying "God bless you" just means "May God do His will in you." Asking God to forgive Trino felt like too much of a leap for me, but asking him to do His will in him made perfect sense. All I needed was to ask God to bless Trino and God would take care of the rest. That I could live with. So it became my daily prayer: "God bless Trino."

Those were three of the toughest words I ever remember uttering, especially because they did not bring instant relief. Evidently, the anger that had built up over the years was like a huge boulder that had to be chiseled away one strike at a time. At every church service, I would be at the altar crying those words. I thought the

Lord would grow tired of hearing them, but of course He never did. I repeated them and repeated them until slowly, their sharp angles started to soften and I was able to utter them without tears or hatred or pain. They became words.

With the passing of time, my prayer changed and it became more like Christ's: "God forgive Trino, for he knew not what he did."

After several weeks of this, my spirit began to feel a release. I could breathe easier, and while I could never erase what Trino had done, slowly, my thoughts were starting to center on reflection and introspection instead of hatred and bitterness. The storm that had been in my soul tempered down to a calm, peaceful lake.

When I did think of Trino, it now included a dream that one day he would be totally reconciled with God. I had read the story of Saul, who once inflicted harm on Christians, including Stephen. He eventually became the Apostle Paul, who spread the gospel to the nations. I envisioned such a change for Trino. I imagined that he would become a man who, after being an abuser, someone who was capable of inflicting such pain on other human beings, would become a new man and a powerful witness: a man of God. His reconciliation would show millions of people across the world that God loves each and every one of them, no matter what they have done.

It is a dream that I hold on to until this day.

I was so grateful to have received God's guidance during this transformative time, for I needed all the strength I could gather to face what was coming.

eleven

face-to-face

One day in January 2006—just a few months after I turned my life over to God—I was having lunch with my friend Gladyz at NORM's on Lakewood Boulevard in Bellflower. I hadn't seen Gladyz in a while and we were catching up. I was still in the middle of dealing with the aftermath of my relationship with Pedro, and Gladyz, who has been with me through thick and thin, was helping me sort through my feelings.

Suddenly my phone rang. It was Pedro. I picked up and soon enough we were in the middle of an argument. As I was talking to Pedro, I looked up from our table for a moment and right then and there I just froze. I felt all the blood drain from my face and I could barely breathe. Gladyz noticed that something was going on and quickly she asked me:

"What's wrong, Rosie? What's the matter?"

I couldn't speak.

Just a few tables away, I had seen Trino.

He looked different, but it didn't take more than a split second for me to know it was him. I couldn't move, I couldn't say anything. All I could do was stare. I couldn't believe my eyes. His nose was different, he had shorter hair, and in general he looked thicker. But it was him, I was sure.

Pedro was screaming his head off through the phone but I could no longer hear him. I sat there, frozen, for what felt like hours but must have been seconds. Trino must have felt my stare because suddenly he looked up and stared me in the eyes. He must have recognized me immediately because right away he got up, pulled some money out of his pocket, and set it on the table. There was a woman sitting at the table with him and he didn't even stop to say a word to her; he just got up and left, walking right past me. I think I held my breath the whole time, I was so shocked.

"Are you okay?" Gladyz insisted.

It wasn't until Trino was out of sight that I managed to finally say something to her: "Go get his plates, go get his plates, Gladyz."

"Why?"

"That's Trino. We need to get him."

Gladyz ran to catch him but it was too late—he had already left the parking lot.

I was so angry. I was convinced that I had made so much progress. I thought I had gotten better but the truth was, I wasn't ready just yet. I was still that little girl who froze. Just like I did as a child in the mobile home. I thought I was over it but I really wasn't.

I started to cry. Like in so many difficult times of my life, the only person I wanted to talk to was Lupe. I called him right away.

"Rosa, what's wrong?" he asked as soon as he heard me sobbing on the phone.

"I'm so dumb, Lupe. I'm so sorry. I'm so, so sorry." I couldn't stop crying.

"It's okay, Rosa. Just tell me. What happened?"

"I saw Trino. . . . But I froze. . . . I froze and . . . I couldn't catch him," I sobbed. "Please don't be mad at me."

Lupe tried to calm me down. "It's okay, Sister, it's okay, baby. Don't you worry," he said. Then after a pause, he asked: "Do you know if the restaurant has security cameras? The good news is that now we know he's in the area and you know what he looks like."

Lupe. Always so smart. Of course he would think to ask whether there were any security cameras.

While Gladyz went to find out, I phoned Chay. As ashamed as I felt for having missed the opportunity to catch Trino, I had to tell her.

"I'm so sorry, Sister," I said as soon as she picked up. "Please forgive me!"

"Sister! Sister, calm down," she said. "Why would I need to forgive you? What happened?"

I explained.

"Don't cry," she said once I told her the whole story. "Everything happens for a reason. Do you remember his face?"

"Yes, clearly," I told her. "He looks younger. I think he's had a face-lift. His hair is cut shorter and is pitch black. And he is thicker."

"Great!" Chay exclaimed. "We are going to catch him and you will be able to identify him."

By this time, I didn't hate him anymore. Yet for years I had planned the perfect words I would say if I ever saw him. I wanted him to know that I was a strong woman. He had not crushed me. This was a speech I had rehearsed countless times in my mind, but that plan fell by the wayside.

About five months after that fateful day when I stumbled into church and reconnected with God our savior, I got a call from Chay. I was at choir practice when the phone rang and because

Chay and I usually texted, I knew it had to be something important. We talked for a little bit and then she asked me:

"Sister, do you think it's time to tell other people what really
happened to you?"

"Yes," I answered without hesitation.

"Do you think you're ready to do it?"

From the moment I told the truth to my family at the age of
sixteen, I had barely spoken of it—at least not in any detail. For a
long time, the thought of talking about my abuse in front of the
people who loved me most, let alone strangers, was absolutely unbearable. Chay and I had talked about the importance of speaking
up about these kinds of things and how it affects so many women
but I just wasn't in a place where I could even process what it had
meant for me. The damage was so deep that it was still too hard
to talk about.

But after all the changes that had taken place over the past five
months, after all the soul-searching and learning to forgive myself
and love myself for who I am, I knew I was ready. Speaking up
about what had happened to me was more important than my own
pride or fear of humiliation. Sexual abuse shouldn't exist and the
more we talk about it and show girls and boys all around the world
that it's okay to speak up and that they're not alone, the better off
we will all be as a society. As a young girl I had spent hours and
hours watching TV, hoping someone would talk about it. Now I
had the opportunity to take a stand and do just that.

Chay wasn't yet a superstar, but her music was very popular; her albums were already selling hundreds of thousands of
units and her songs were constantly on the Spanish radio charts.
Coming out on Spanish-language TV to talk about such a taboo
subject—especially within the Mexican-American community—as
sexual abuse, would be putting her career at risk. Plenty of people

tried to dissuade her, saying that the public would not like her anymore for airing her dirty laundry in public but Chay was determined. She wanted to talk about what had happened; she wanted to show the world that sexual abuse is not something one has to endure alone.

"One reason I want to do this is because I want to reach some frightened child who this might be happening to right now. When that child hears your ordeal, I want her to be encouraged enough to know that if you can get through it, she can too."

But Chay also had a second reason: she hoped that being on TV would help us get information on where Trino was, not only for us to bring him to justice, but also so her kids could see their father again. My niece, Jacqie, was eight when her father disappeared. She didn't really understand all the circumstances of his disappearance and had begged to see him from that day on. She was now a young woman of sixteen. Chay would reassure her, "I promise we are going to find your dad, and when he is put in jail, I will take you to visit him. I promise."

Chay spoke to Jacqie and Chiquis and they too were ready to talk about their abuse in public, so Chay booked us for a sit-down interview on *Escándalo TV* with the one and only Charytín.

The interview took place at Chay's house in Corona, and it feels like ages ago when I think about it: the four of us squeezed together on the big couch in her living room, answering question after question. It was the first time Chiquis, Jacqie, and I did a TV interview and we were all so nervous. Chay was nervous too, but as always, she was holding it together for the rest of us. But despite the difficulty of the subject, Charytín somehow managed to make us feel comfortable and we were able to talk in all honesty about what had happened.

By the time the interview had ended, I was so proud of how far we had come. The experience had been terrifying, but I knew we were making a difference in other peoples' lives and that meant the world to me. After so many years of wallowing in my own self-pity, thinking no one in the world had it harder than me, it felt extraordinary to be able to do something meaningful, something important that would help other girls going through the same thing I had gone through, or even worse. At one point during the interview, Chay explained that what motivated her most to do the show was that Chiquis had come to her one day saying that four of her five friends had been sexually abused, and there were some girls whose mothers didn't believe them. I knew my journey had been very difficult, but I felt blessed to have a sister who believed me the instant I told her. Learning that some girls didn't even have that made me realize even more the importance of what we were doing.

The interview aired the first week of April 2006 but we weren't quite prepared for the firestorm that followed. The media went crazy with the news. Some people applauded Chay and us for our bravery; others accused Chay of just using the abuse as a publicity stunt to sell more records. For better or for worse, we had gotten people to talk about it and that, at least, was a triumph for us.

A couple of weeks later, there was so much buzz about the topic that K-Love radio, one of the most popular stations in Los Angeles, asked Chay and me to come in for an interview.

The eight a.m. host asked us to give an update on the sexual abuse story. We let the audience know that our brother Lupe had set up a fund to offer a fifty-thousand-dollar reward for information leading to the arrest of Trino.

Seconds later, the phones started ringing off the hook.

Plenty of people called up saying they had new information. At first we got excited but quickly realized that most of the tips were either irrelevant or they happened years earlier. But we didn't lose hope. We took call after call, hoping to unearth even a small clue that might help us in finding Trino.

In the end, we received two very important calls that day. The first was from an FBI agent. He had heard our story and was moved by it. He was from Florida but he was in Southern California working on an unrelated case. He had caught the interview on his car radio and he immediately felt the need to reach out to us.

"I am a Christian," he said, "and felt in my heart that I needed to call you. I want to offer you my help."

He was a federal agent and could therefore not be involved in a state case—helping us, in fact, put him at risk of losing his job—but he still wanted to help us in any way he could. He couldn't, of course, tell us his name but he asked us to call him "Angel"—he was our angel sent from God. And from that moment on, Angel stayed by our side.

The second call came from a woman who, as soon as she came on the air, said, "Jenni, I really love you and want to talk with you off the air." We were surprised, but there was nothing to lose so my sister agreed and jotted down the woman's number. She phoned her back later that morning. Sure enough, she had something interesting to say.

"Jenni, I am Trino's neighbor," she explained over the phone. "I've seen him drunk, bragging about being your husband—and about the kids. One night, he was even boasting of those terrible things you have accused him of."

Chay was floored and asked her to continue. "I can tell you where he is, but I really don't want to get involved. My husband told me to stay out of it and that it's none of my business." She paused. "Please, I just want to help but I'm not going to give you my real name."

"I understand. You have my word, and I appreciate what you are doing," replied Chay.

The woman then gave us Trino's address, which Chay wrote down. She thanked the woman profusely. "But what about the reward?" she asked.

The woman hesitated. "I don't want all the money, but we do need ten thousand dollars because my mother is sick and we want to get her to Mexico."

Chay thanked her again for her help. If it hadn't been for this woman, we might still be looking for Trino till this day. Her bravery and her selflessness were determining factors in what was to come.

A couple of days later, Chay asked me to meet the caller at a McDonald's near where she lived in North Corona, just a few miles south of Chay's house in Corona. We were shocked. All that time, Trino had been so close to my sister and we hadn't even known it.

All of a sudden, it made sense—he had stayed so close to Chay because he knew that was the one place we would never expect him to be. The confirmation that Trino was so near, far from frightening me, brought me peace. I felt as if God had placed him in my hands as soon as I was able to give Him all my hate, anger, and desire for revenge. I felt calm and collected, clear-minded and focused—we weren't playing hide-and-seek anymore; we were playing chess. Anger makes you lose control and I knew I needed love, strength, and a sound mind to finish the game.

We all agreed that it would be good for me to be the one to go to meet her in person. Not only was I the person who had seen him most recently, but also I had reached a point in my life where I was at peace with my past. I felt tremendous strength inside me and each step that brought us closer to Trino also brought me closer to my healing. I no longer wanted to find Trino because I was angry; I wanted to find justice, especially for the children who have never received justice.

So on another beautiful sunny Southern California day, I set out on the long drive from Lakewood to Corona. Part of me was nervous that the whole thing might be a scam, but I was excited that we were getting so close to finding justice. From the moment I sat down to talk to the lady, I knew she was sincere. She was terrified of being involved and by the detailed description she gave me of Trino, I knew that it was really him. She described him as having dark hair, medium build, and he had two kids. She said he was a kind and charismatic man and that she had never had problems with him as a neighbor. In fact, her son was friendly with Trino's stepson, whose name she mentioned in passing. I knew it had to be Trino because no fan would ever know that name. That's when I knew for sure. So, in good faith, I gave her an envelope containing ten thousand dollars in one hundred dollar bills.

As soon as I got into the car after meeting her, I called Angel and said, "I know where Trino lives. It's in Corona." My voice was shaking as I told him because I had a feeling in my gut that this time we were really going to find him. Not only did we finally have the right information as well as the help we needed; this time *I* was ready.

Angel was excited with the news. To him, this was more than a big break.

"What's the address?" he asked immediately. "On my free time, I will stake out the house with a camera. I'll interview the neighbors as discreetly as possible and will let you know what I find."

Sure enough, that's what he did. For a couple of weeks, Angel hung around Trino's neighborhood getting the lay of the land. He met Trino's neighbors, observed his comings and goings—as well as those of his family—and from all the information he gathered, it became clear that it was, indeed, Trino. Angel would call me from time to time to fill me in on the situation and the whole time I was on pins and needles, waiting to find out what would be our next move.

"I made a video of him throwing out his trash," he told me one day. "Let's meet somewhere and I'll show it to you so you can tell me if it's really him."

I hopped into my car right away. As I drove to meet with Angel at a Starbucks in the Long Beach Town Center, my mind flew back to that day, months earlier, when I was sitting at NORM's in Bellflower on the phone with my sister and in tears because I had failed to catch Trino. "Everything happens for a reason," she had said. And she was right. If it hadn't been for the fact that I had seen him just a few months earlier, I might have not been able to identify him. I hadn't been foolish for not catching him; it was all part of God's plan.

It didn't take more than five seconds for me to know it was Trino. There he was, living a normal life, taking out some bags of garbage. It seemed so surreal to me that this person I'd been thinking about for all these years, this man who had hurt my sister, my nieces, and me so deeply was still roaming around, a free man. What was interesting, however, was that as he was throwing out the trash he seemed to be glancing around, a person with his guard up—a man with a guilty conscience.

I looked up and told Angel: "I am one hundred percent sure that's him."

"Good," he said. "I'll take the necessary steps to see that this case is reopened."

Angel called the Los Angeles Police Department and gave them all the information he had found out. That was when he learned that the Long Beach detective who had been investigating the case nine years prior (nine years!) had passed away. They were unable to locate the records, which meant that with the detective's death, the entire case had faded into oblivion. No wonder our calls weren't being returned. No wonder no one was following up on the case. It was a frustrating discovery, but now, with a new team looking at the fresh evidence, significant progress was finally being made.

On Saturday, April 22, 2006, my phone rang. It was Angel.

"Are you ready?" he asked.

"For what?"

"Today is the day we arrest Trino. Do you want to be present?"

Of course I did! I was nervous, but overjoyed. Finally, after all those years of praying, after all those years of suffering, Trino was going to be brought before justice. My heart had accepted God and I no longer craved revenge; all I needed at this point was closure. I needed to know that Trino was going to face us for what he had done. I also wanted other victims to see that justice is possible and share our victory as if it was theirs. I wanted to bring hope to the hopeless.

I couldn't wait to tell my sister. She was out of town doing a show, but I knew she would celebrate as soon as she found out.

"This is a day I've been waiting for! Justice is going to be served," she said. She wasn't able to come with me for the arrest, but my mother bravely offered to join me. Even though Chay was far away, I could feel her strength and her support. She had promised to stand by me no matter what and that's exactly what she did.

A few hours later, Angel came by to pick us up. We drove from

Long Beach to Corona in an unmarked van with dark, tinted windows. We would be able to see Trino, but he wouldn't be able to see us. I was pleased about that, because I was fearful of what might happen if he knew I was there.

We drove to the address we had gotten from the woman on the radio and the cops jumped out of several police cars that came screeching to a halt. Trino was standing outside his house, peacefully watering his lawn. The police officers rushed up to him and when they showed him the arrest warrant, he just bowed his head and complied with the officers as they told him to put his hands behind his back and they clamped on the handcuffs. It was as if he had been waiting for it all along.

A few seconds later, Trino's wife—who had been with him since his split from Chay—came out of the house yelling and screaming: "This isn't true! No! He's an innocent man! Don't take him, please, don't take him!" She was sobbing uncontrollably. The police had to hold her away.

As the police officers walked Trino to their vehicle, his daughter, who was about eight years old at the time, came running out of the house. She was crying and begging, "Please don't take my daddy! Please don't take him away!"

Seeing his daughter and his wife suffer like that just broke my heart. I hated that I was contributing to breaking up a family and, in all honesty, if I had been in either of their shoes, I would have probably been just as distraught. And the fact was, I knew how sweet Trino could be. I knew he was an attentive dad and how hard it was to believe that he could be capable of such a thing. I felt particularly bad for Trino's youngest daughter. Just like Chiquis, Jacqie, and Michael, she was losing her father and it tore me apart to see that unfold before my eyes.

On the other hand, I had to genuinely ask myself, *Had he done* to his youngest daughter what he did to Chiquis, Jacqie, and me? I couldn't help thinking that she was about the same age I was when he started the abuse and it was a very real possibility that he was either doing it, or about to start doing it to her. We simply couldn't allow that to happen again and that thought alone kept me going the following months, especially at times when I felt myself go weak in the knees.

The police officers put Trino in a pickup truck that was about ten feet from where we were sitting inside the van. I was able to catch a long glimpse of him and what I saw wasn't the Trino I'd been terrified of for all those years. I saw a small, weak man who looked ashamed, with his head hung low. A deeply flawed man.

In that instant, I realized I no longer felt hate for Trino, but God's compassion. After all those years of suffering and the many months of rediscovering the power of God's love, compassion, and forgiveness, I no longer held an ounce of hatred toward Trino in my heart. For so many years, I had lived in a prison of his making—one of pain, depression, and anger. But now I was free.

Without saying a word, I watched as they took him away. My mom and I had remained silent during the entire arrest. About five minutes into the drive home, all of a sudden, I started screaming for joy. The reality of what had just happened hit me full force: justice really exists! At the top of my lungs I yelled, "Glory to God! You are so good!"

Mom was crying with happiness.

Even Angel couldn't contain his joy. "This is why I love my job. For moments like this."

twelve

on trial

Trino was behind bars, but our ordeal was far from being over.

In the days following the arrest, Trino's bail was set at one million dollars—given his history, the authorities were concerned that he was a flight risk. On the other hand, Chay's children were having a hard time dealing with what was unfolding. They loved their dad and didn't want anything to happen to him. Chiquis, in particular, was having a very hard time because Trino's entire family had been calling her a liar for years and she was understandably shaken. I felt terrible for what they were going through and so did Chay—as always, she was there to support them every step of the way. Chay had her hands full with what has going on at home so she asked me to handle, as much as possible, the requests coming in from the court, the attorneys, and the detectives concerning the investigation.

"You studied law and know the lingo," she told me. "You take care of this." She wanted to concentrate on her family and making sure the kids were all right.

We began talking with the authorities in late May 2006, and a preliminary hearing was scheduled for the next month at the Long Beach Superior Court.

Trino got himself a high-profile attorney, Richard Poland, who had an outstanding record of winning cases of this kind. On our side was a court-appointed attorney, Deputy District Attorney Mark Burnley, who had just come out of law school and had never defended a case like this before. It was David versus Goliath; however, we had little say in the matter since it was ultimately a California state case: The People v. Jose Trinidad Marín.

In one of the preliminary hearings, the two attorneys argued back and forth as to whether media would be allowed at the trial. Trino's lawyers wanted cameras in the courtroom—even though, ironically, he also claimed that the accusations were no more than a publicity stunt orchestrated by the Riveras. On our side, we were adamant in requesting that the media not be present. Chay's popularity had continued to grow over the years and as it was, the scandal was already plastered all over the news.

Thank God, the judge ultimately agreed with us—no cameras would be allowed inside but journalists, like any other person interested in the case, would be able to attend.

The circus was about to begin.

The trial lasted over twelve months. For twelve months, we had to go to court about once a month and for twelve months the entire Rivera family—my parents, my brothers, my sister, and my nieces and nephews—were there to support us. Chay cleared her schedule to make sure she was absolutely free on every court date, and so did my brothers. It was a very difficult year for me, but knowing that my family was standing by my side and helping me get through the aftermath of the one secret I kept from them all those years made me realize just how blessed I am.

I truly am.

The year before we found Trino, Chay had been going through a particularly difficult time with her second husband, Juan. There was a jewelry store at the time that had a slogan—"Women of the World, Raise Your Right Hand"—that meant to tell women that they didn't have to wait for a man to buy them a diamond ring. Chay loved the idea of doing away with men and getting herself what she needed, so she went ahead and bought herself a big beautiful diamond ring that she wore all the time. We took to calling it her "Victory Ring" since it symbolized how she had made it—all on her own.

The day before the trial started, Chay and I were hanging out and trying to imagine how it was going to unfold, and we were giving each other courage and strength for what was to come.

Suddenly Chay slipped the Victory Ring off her finger and said, "This represents a promise I personally made to keep myself strong. Now you need to have it, Sister. I want you to wear it during the trial—and I know it will help give you the strength to make it through."

And I did. I wore it every day of those twelve months and I had never felt stronger.

Every single time we had to be in court, the courthouse was packed. Trino's family sat on one side, the Riveras sat on the other, and the few spots that were left were occupied by hungry members of the press who reported on every single detail of the trial. Before Trino fled nearly a decade earlier, he had been charged with nine felonies—including counts of a lewd act with a child under the age of fourteen, aggravated sexual assault, and continuous sexual abuse of a minor. Those were the same charges being brought against him at the trial.

Trino's attorney made several motions to dismiss the case, but they were all rejected. The first months went by and a number of individuals gave depositions. But when the time came for Chiquis and me to testify, we were brought in separately. Since we were both making charges against Trino, neither of us could be present while the other spoke. I was now twenty-five, and Chiquis was twenty-one. Nine years had gone by since that fateful day when we told Chay everything.

I was terrified. Even though I had been waiting eighteen years for this moment, this was going to be the first time I spoke about being molested in such detail. Of course, I had talked to therapists and counselors at length; we had also done the TV interview where we talked about the psychological consequences of what happened, but never before had I really shared any of the gruesome details. The idea of having to do that in front of my family—let alone other people I didn't even know yet—was horrifying. Even the thought of saying it all in front of Trino made me nervous. I was embarrassed to have to share all the details and it made me feel ashamed and guilty for what had happened. It was easier for me to forgive Trino than myself.

Lupe, always the guardian of my fears, knew exactly what was going through my mind. He told me to keep my eyes focused on the attorneys and the judge—he told me to look at him—but not to even glance at Trino.

The night before I was to testify, I closed my eyes and prayed. "Please God, speak through me," I asked Him.

I could hear His response: "I want you to know that you will not take the stand without Me. You will be on My lap—the way you used to sit on your daddy's lap at the kitchen table. A time when you knew you were loved."

Then I opened my Bible and before me was Psalm 27: *The Lord is my light and my salvation; whom shall I fear? The Lord is the strength of my life; of whom shall I be afraid?*

"The Lord is going to help me," I said to myself. "The Holy Spirit is going to tell me what to say."

When I walked in the chamber and was called to the witness stand, I refused to look at Trino because I knew that no matter what his reaction was, it would affect me. So I did what I had to do to keep it together: I just focused my eyes on Lupe, and remembered that nothing bad could happen to me since I was sitting on God's lap.

I told the facts as clearly as I could remember them and felt I was doing a good job. But when Trino's attorney began his cross-examination, I wasn't sure what would happen. I was afraid he'd ask me things I couldn't remember. And even if you are one hundred percent sure of what happened, when you're sitting in front of a judge, a jury, and an attorney who's pressing you with difficult questions, you still get nervous. The whole time I kept wondering, *Are the jurors going to believe me? Am I remembering enough?* Sure enough, Trino's attorney pressed me about minor details I had forgotten, but I answered every question as honestly as possible. And if it was something I definitely couldn't remember, I simply replied, "I don't know."

The most difficult part was recounting everything Trino had done to me in front of my father. With every detail I gave, I knew I was breaking my father's heart.

When Chiquis was called to the stand, I was escorted out of

the room, but I was praying for her since I knew that everything I was feeling, she had to be feeling a hundred times worse. I knew how much she loved her dad—probably as much as I loved mine—and I couldn't even begin to imagine the pain of having to testify against him.

My whole family stayed inside the courtroom supporting Chiquis while I waited outside all alone. The hallway felt dark and lonely and the air was still. Everything was quiet; you could hear a pin drop. Yet no matter how hard I strained my ears, I couldn't hear Chiquis's voice. I didn't actually want to hear what she was saying—I knew it would be too much to bear—but the silence was maddening. To keep my mind from trying to imagine the things Trino might have done to her, I focused my mind on everything around me—the hardness of the bench, the cool marble floor, the painting on the wall—while I read and reread Psalm 27 to keep myself calm.

When my family filed out after Chiquis's questioning, I could see the sorrow and grief on their faces. Chiquis was crying, and Chay was holding her tight. Pastor Pete whispered, "Rosie, it was worse than what he did to you." He hugged me and said, "It's going to be okay. God is going to restore us all."

We all walked out of the courthouse in shock and in silence.

The next day, a medical doctor took the stand and spoke of what he found when he examined Jacqie at the age of eight. He testified that the evidence showed that she had been molested when she was very young, most likely between the ages of two and four.

Trino chose not to say a word during the trial. For the most part, he kept a straight face and showed no emotion. Sometimes he would shake his head at us, as if in disappointment, but I knew it was nothing but another mind trick, so I did my best to ignore him. At every possible instance, Richard Poland kept hammering away that Trino was a good man, that he had always been a good dad, and this was nothing more than a publicity stunt by the spotlight-hungry Rivera family trying to get in the news.

Months went by and one day in October 2006, we found that Trino had posted bail. We were shocked. How could that be? How on earth could he have raised so much money? Then we heard he owned some property and had either sold it or put a lien against it.

Upon learning this, of course our biggest fear was that Trino would pull another disappearing act. He had been on the run for nine years; what would stop him from running now? But our fears were appeased when the next court date came around, and Trino not only showed up—he was looking sharp in a suit and tie. He seemed confident that he was going to win the case.

Trino's family was convinced of his innocence. They were all there to support him and at every chance they had, they made sure to let us know. Trino's family had never liked Chay. He came from a family of all sisters, so to them he was a god and of course Chay was unworthy of such perfection. The fact that on top of it now she had become a famous recording artist and she was accusing him of sexually molesting minors made them despise her even more.

By the time the hearing came to an end that day, tensions were running high. Trino was acting cocky, and my brothers didn't like it one bit. As he walked past our side of the courtroom, Trino looked over at Lupe and said something to him. Chay's son, Michael, who was sitting next to Lupe, overheard what he said and without giving it a second thought, he threw himself on top of Trino and punched him in the face.

"Don't you disrespect my uncle!" he said.

Instead of striking back at Michael, Trino landed a punch on Lupe. Now both Lupe and Michael were going after Trino and soon enough all hell broke loose. Someone tried to separate Trino, Michael, and Lupe but the pacifying efforts came too late—behind him, World War III had erupted. The Maríns and the Riveras were throwing punches left and right. One of Trino's sisters hit my sister in the face and Chay being Chay, she hit her right back. One of Trino's aunts began pulling Chiquis's hair, calling her a liar. My mother and I started yelling, "Stop! Stop! Please stop!" To this day, I thank God for the fact my brother Juan was running late and wasn't around for the fight. If he had been there, things would have really gotten out of hand.

If I hadn't been a believer, I would have probably had someone on the floor but now all I wanted was peace. The members of Trino's family were innocent bystanders; they too were victims of his lies. Yet I also understood my family's pain and frustration erupting from being trapped in a volcano for the nine years we had been looking for him. No one was to blame but Trino, and now he had more than three victims. All the Riveras and the Maríns had counts of lies, pain, and shame against him yet unfortunately those couldn't be taken before a judge . . . so they tried to take justice into their own hands.

Twenty security guards rushed in and they were just about to arrest us all when my brother Pete—wise Pastor Pete—arrived and pleaded with the police not to arrest anyone. Before long, both families admitted fault and promised to behave in the future. Still, the judge gave us a warning and said that if anything like that ever happened again, we'd all end up in jail.

From that point on, there was extra security assigned, not just in the courtroom but in the entire building. The Marín family entered through one door, and the Riveras through another. They even kept us separated in the hallways.

Finally, the day came for closing arguments. Richard Poland pleaded with the six-man, six-woman jury to acquit Trino of the charges of aggravated sexual assault on Chiquis and me. I'll never forget how he stood in front of the jury and asked them: "What can be worse than being a child molester? Maybe being falsely accused of being a child molester."

To him, our allegations were nothing more than a publicity stunt orchestrated by my sister in order to make it big in the music industry. I couldn't believe my ears. To think that a mother would put her daughter—let alone her sister—through an ordeal like this just to sell more records? Really? What kind of monster did they think she was? Could the jury even buy something like this?

On our side, the district attorney stuck to the facts. He reminded the jurors that based on the evidence set forth throughout the trial, it was clear that Trinidad Marín was guilty of what he was being accused of. He had taken advantage of us at a young age, and had used threats to get away with it. "Trinidad Marín is a predator," he said, "and highly deserving of the highest stigma of sexual molestation."

Then the judge gave her instructions to the jury. Dressed in a pin-striped suit and wearing a very serious expression, Trino sat motionless in the courtroom. After only a few hours of deliberation, the jury came back with a verdict. Their decision was unanimous: they found him guilty on eight of nine counts.

Trino was taken away in cuffs while his family cried in disbelief. I felt terrible for them, but most of all I felt terrible for his children. They had never done anything to deserve this. I had lost my childhood and my innocence. But that day, my sister's children were losing their father for a second time and my heart broke in a million pieces.

Justice was served, but it was bittersweet.

Trino's sentencing was set for June 20, 2007. As the date drew closer, I felt the Lord asking me: "Daughter, what do you want for Trino?"

But I didn't have an answer. For years I had wanted Trino to be punished for what he had done, but now that I was faced with the reality of it, I was left with no words. What price could be placed on my eighteen years of suffering? How could that be measured? What was my childhood worth? I simply didn't know. All I could think of was Chiquis, Jacqie, and Michael and how sad it was for them to have to grow up without a father; how sad it was that all this had happened; how sad it was that Trino's life had come down to this. I also felt terrible for his other two kids . . . but maybe, just maybe, I had saved his daughter from sexual abuse. Statistics show that sexual molesters get worse with time—what Trino did to Chiquis was much worse than what he did to me, so I couldn't help thinking that maybe he had hurt—or would hurt—the next child more.

Even though for so many years, I had been convinced of the contrary, I knew that seeing Trino incarcerated would not bring joy to my heart or soul. Yes, the fact that he had been confronted with his acts and brought before justice helped me heal and now I could breathe easier; I was at peace. But I knew now that his punishment, though necessary, would give me no satisfaction.

Then I heard God ask, "What is justice to you?"

Again, I didn't know, but I responded, "What I really and truly want is for his heart to change toward You; for him to repent for what he did and acknowledge the truth." I realized that I didn't need to hear Trino say "I'm sorry" to me, but told the Lord, "Whatever it takes for him to be in a cell alone and have an encounter and reconcile with You, that's what I want," I said. I didn't care if it took one day, six months, or forty years.

My words were completely sincere. I hoped with all my heart that he too would find solace in God and hopefully one day become his witness. I prayed for the difference he could make in people's lives if only he shared with others his own truth and showed them that despite all of the pain and suffering he caused, despite all his wrongdoings, God loves him. God will always love him.

At the final sentencing, we had a chance to speak before the judge. This time Trino was wearing prison orange again.

I had written out what I was going to say: "I lost my innocence when I was eight years old. From that moment forward, I lost my trust in men, in myself, and in the world. I cannot say what a proper sentence would be in this case. I don't know what a person's childhood is worth. I could no longer look my niece in the eye because of the horrible guilt I felt. If I had spoken out about the abuse when it happened, this may never have happened to Chiquis."

At this, the judge said to me, "All the guilt belongs to Marín, not you."

Chay's son, Michael, never said a word during the trial, but at the sentencing, he looked directly at his father and told him, "Dad, all I want to say is 'good-bye,' because I never had a chance to do so."

Hearing those words was heartbreaking. Especially since he was just five years old when his father deserted him—and Trino never once called or tried to contact him. We later found out that Trino would look for Chiquis—he'd even go to her high school so he could see her from a distance—but he never once sought out his son.

The last to speak was Chiquis. She looked at her father and said, "Daddy, we didn't have to get to this point. None of us wanted this. We just need you to acknowledge the fact that we are not liars. But now that we are here, I want you to know that I forgive you and that I love you."

When she spoke those words, I looked directly at Trino, thinking this was his moment to show some remorse; to show Chiquis he loved her. But the instant Chiquis said "I love you," he just rolled his eyes and looked away.

I could have killed him. How could he do that to his own daughter? And even if he didn't care about her, how could he be so royally *stupid* to do that in front of the judge? My poor Chiquis, nothing could have been more hurtful to her, and you could see it written on her face. As much as she tried, she couldn't win the love of her father. My heart sank and I said, "Lord, do what you have to do."

Superior Court Judge Joan Comparet-Cassani told everyone in attendance, "I've heard everything I need." She stated that she considered child molestation among the three most horrendous crimes—just below murder and torture—and added, "To molest your own child is a betrayal of the worst kind."

Then she sentenced Jose Trinidad Marín to thirty-one years to life in prison without the possibility of parole. He was forty-three years old at the time, which meant he cannot be released until he is at least seventy-four years of age.

The sounds of wailing from his family filled the courtroom as a beaten, dejected Trino was escorted back to jail.

. . .

Since his trial had been such a high-profile case and it involved child molestation, Trino was given extra protection in prison. Some inmates sent us messages to let us know that if Chay paid their families a certain amount of money, they would be willing to take Trino out. Chay was horrified and she of course said no.

A few months into his incarceration, the Marín family contacted Jacqie to let her know that her father wanted to see her. He wanted her to come visit him in prison. Jacqie, whose heart was broken since the day her father picked up and vanished when she was eight years old, was excited at the prospect of seeing him. Understandably, she missed her dad and really wanted to go.

Chay, true to her belief never to keep a father from his children, felt the timing was right. Regardless of what had happened, now that Tino was behind bars, she willing to let her kids have a relationship with their father. So she agreed, but with one condition: he had to see all three of his children. Trino's response came back a few days later: he would see everyone except Chiquis.

Once again, he broke her heart.

Chay wasn't about to let him get away with hurting her baby girl again. "If he doesn't see all three of you, then he sees none of you."

The kids agreed, and to this day, they have not seen their father.

Life went on. With Trino sentenced and in jail, we all felt that we could finally close this chapter and move on. While the effect of Trino's actions will always be a part of my life, the fact that there was justice did make a difference. I was able to put my demons to rest and I have been able to heal, forgive, and move on. I am adorned with justice and those are the best jewels. Yet everything I have lived through up until this moment is a part of who I am. Everything I have done, everything I have felt, everything I have received and experienced—everything has made me into the person I am today, and I finally like who I am.

That's why I'm not upset at God for the sexual abuse. Now, I'm at a point in my life where I can accept it and be thankful I became the person I am today. I know He didn't allow it to happen. I know that we are in a fallen world where people make mistakes and people sin. The sexual abuse was Trino's sin. Mine was having an abortion. Both Trino and I need forgiveness. We both need to repent. I still think my crime was bigger because I took a life while he didn't. But I've forgiven myself and I've forgiven Trino—I know that God will help us find the purpose in what we have been given to live.

As time passed and I thought more and more about these things, making sense of my innermost feelings, I felt the urge to unburden my heart to Trino. He had heard my courtroom testimony, but I still had things I wanted to tell him, so in early 2012 I decided to put my thoughts down on paper.

Trino:
Please do not tear this up! Please take the time to read it. I beg of you, for your sake and mine. I mean no harm; I just need to tell you the things that I have held in my heart for all of these years. I pray you keep reading. I went to the Paramount Swap Meet today and as I pulled into the parking lot, I felt an odd sensation in the pit of my stomach. An old familiar feeling washed over my being. My old friend Sadness joined me.

As I walked down the rows and rows of merchandise for

*sale, I regressed further and further back into my childhood.
I tried to think of all the beautiful memories I had of playing
with my brothers, Lupe and Juan, or of my mom and
dad working together and building an empire out of
nothing . . . but, as usual, all my childhood memories
led back to you.*

*For eighteen years, from the age of eight to twenty-six,
I thought of you every single day of my life. I do not believe
there is another person in this world who has thought of you
as much as I have.*

*In good moments, when I feel strong, compassionate,
and kind, I think of you. In bad moments, when I feel weak,
ugly, and worthless, my thoughts are of you. Every time
I hear the word sex, your face is in my mind. Today, I feel
your spirit near me and sometimes I think I see you in
other men.*

*I have always wondered if you ever gave a thought to
me, that young blond girl whose life you permanently
scarred the summer of 1989. Have you ever taken three
minutes to consider the effect you had on an innocent
child and how the weight of the whole world fell on her
shoulders?*

*I have a hundred questions, but I have finally come to
grips with the fact that I may never get the answers I
desperately needed growing up. I can live with unanswered
questions, but I refuse to live in this deafening silence.
Finally, you will know what I have endured for so long.
I have regained the voice you stole from me, and now
I direct it back to you.*

*Trino, I strongly believe God has confined you to the
four walls of your prison so that you can no longer run*

away from me. You cannot ignore or hide from my thoughts, my feelings, and my truth. Our truth.

As an eight-year-old girl chasing after her beloved older sister Chay, I loved you. I loved you as her husband. I thought of you as my older brother and I admired the deep passionate love she felt for you. My sister was, and is, my hero. She could do no wrong in my eyes. Chay was the smartest women I had ever met and if she chose you as a husband, then you had to be a good man. Right? I lived to please Chay and receive her love. Everything I did and said was to make her smile and laugh. If she loved you, so did I. If she defended you, I defended you. When she forgave you for hitting her, I forgave you as well. The pure heart of a child assumed that if she loved me, and you loved her, then you would love me also. Right?

All I knew was love. Being the baby of my family meant all I received was love and protection. It was their duty to take care of me and love me; Daddy's orders. I thought that everyone would, especially in my family. You were my sister's husband and an older brother who would protect me. Wrong! I was dead wrong!

The first recollection I have of you and my childhood was in Chiquis's empty room inside the Carson, California, mobile home. Visiting Chay meant two great things: First, I got to spend time with my sister. And second, I did not have to go work at the hot, dirty swap meet. At every opportunity, I would choose to go to Chay's and avoid the work.

A dark blue rug and a worn-out San Marcos blanket were the furnishings of the room where Chiquis, my very first friend, and I were playing Barbies. Warm rays of sunshine streamed through the open window. I could smell the aroma of the meat sauce for Chay's famous spaghetti and meatballs. It was my favorite dish and she made it for me anytime I asked. Spaghetti has become the symbol for the day that destroyed my life.

When Chiquis and I heard the screaming and cursing coming from the living room we were startled. Then I reminded her that you and Chay fought all the time and would make up any minute. Everything would be okay. She believed me as much as I believed it myself.

The silence after the door slammed was new, so Chiquis and I decided to step outside the room and check out the battle zone. To my surprise you were in the kitchen and Chay was nowhere to be seen. Do you remember that I asked where Chay was and you calmly told me that she went to the store to buy something for dinner? You reassured us that everything would be fine and told us to go and play. Chiquis and I happily went back to our dolls and fantasy world.

After a while, you entered the room and told Chiquis to leave. She began to protest, but you quickly yelled at her. I was startled and confused as to why Chiquis had to leave, but kept playing in silence. Once my little friend was gone, you told me to lie down on the blanket. I looked up at you, so big and tall, and wondered why.

You kindly explained that we were going to play a new game. I liked games and was excited to learn something new and tell Chiquis all about it. You ordered me to close my eyes, lie down on the blanket, and put the Barbies aside.

Never again would I view those dolls the same. The two blond Barbies were the only witnesses to the heinous

crime that was about to follow me the rest of my life.
I became as silent and frozen as they were. I became a
eight-year-old human Barbie under your power and control.

I was my sister's first living doll but she never intended
for me to be played with like this. I obeyed you, as my
mother had taught me to always obey my elders. My world
faded to black under my eyelids and under your touch. Your
lips came close to my left ear as you whispered, "We are
going to play that we love each other." Love was my
favorite thing in the world so I thought I would really
enjoy this game.

Confusion started to set in as your lips kissed my neck
and your large hands came under the blanket and into my
underwear. Just as you were lying next to me, Chiquis came
in and asked a question that would haunt me for the rest of
my youth. "Are you going to play with her the way you play
with Mommy?"

You yelled at Chiquis to get out and she quickly shut the
door behind her. Now I was sure something was not right.
How could you play the same game with me that you played
with Chay? Would Chay be mad at me for playing her
game? Why couldn't Chiquis play too?

I was terrified of hurting Chay and I opened my mouth
to speak, but you told me not to worry—everything would
be fine.

Despite all the uncertainty, I trusted you and lay there as
you touched me in places I had never before been touched.
It seemed like an eternity, when suddenly you got up and
left, never uttering a word.

Love. That was love. Whatever had just happened meant
you loved me and I loved you. I was scared and bewildered,

but I knew I was loved. I could not wait for Chay to get back home.

I do not remember eating the spaghetti or what time my older sister returned. I have no other memories of that day or any other day with you until the next time you wanted to play the "love game."

After these many years, I can still vividly recall details of the room, your breath, and Chiquis's innocent face. I remember the confusion; it followed me for years to come. To this day, I wondered if you remembered that first encounter. I assume you have blocked it out to protect yourself from a guilty conscious.

Maybe you have fooled your family, your lawyer, and even yourself that this never happened, but today as you read my words you can no longer hide from the truth. You touched my most private parts and robbed me of my innocence.

Now as you read this in your prison cell, all alone, I want you to reflect on that little girl who would never, ever be the same. Remember her big brown eyes and bright smile, because after that first "love" encounter, they faded. You took them with you as you walked out of the room and left me alone and violated. I lost the game that day—and many more that were to follow.

I am writing you my memory just in case you have tried to erase yours. May you think of me every single day as I have thought of you. We are connected, you and I, forever. Whether you loved me or not, I want you to know that as a child, I loved you. All is fair in love and war. Let's see who wins.

—Rosie

I wanted Trino to understand that although I forgave him, I was never going to forget. I sent him my letter but I never received a reply. Even so, writing and sending it offered me a sense of peace. It allowed me to release the deep recesses of my soul and move on with my life. Yes, I had forgiven Trino and turned the justice over to God, but I prayed that somehow he would come face-to-face with the past—as a prerequisite for finding his own forgiveness.

thirteen

loving abel

When my Kassey was about five years old, I began to pray that God would send a man into my life who understood the commitment I had made to Him and was walking down the same path.

There were several guys at church who threw glances in my direction, but Pastor Pete advised, "Don't rush the matter. Give it a couple of years. I feel that you are going to marry a man who has a heart for ministry."

Knowing how bad I was at choosing men, I decided to listen to my brother. After all, our brothers used to always say to Chay and me: "For two smart girls, you guys sure are lousy at picking men." And given our track record up until that moment, I had to admit they were right!

That didn't stop me, however, from begging God every day for a loving husband. Eventually my luck *had* to turn; I knew it. I prayed, "Lord, I'm not good at choosing men, so please pick one for me—a person who will be good to my daughter and who will not hurt her." And to prove to God how much I trusted Him and how much I believed He would send me the right man, I started saving up for my wedding. Every month I would put four hundred dollars aside as a way of showing God, and myself, how much I believed in my future now.

Ever since I'd turned my life over to the Lord, I started to hang out with a new group of friends who were all members of the worship team at church. It wasn't that I'd grown apart from my old friends; it was just that I was having such a good time exploring this new part of my life that I wanted to spend as much time as I could talking and thinking about the Lord. Plus, these were friends who like me didn't drink, or smoke, or curse, so I didn't even feel as if I had to give any explanations. And at this time, when I still had to make an effort to keep temptation at bay, it's what felt right. I could simply be myself.

In the group was a young man by the name of Abel Flores. I had met him early on when I started attending church again and we became friends. I liked him a lot but following Pastor Pete's admonition, I stayed clear of any potential relationship.

But sometimes things happen even when you specifically *don't* want them to happen! One evening, when my friends and I had planned a get-together at a local restaurant, for one reason or another, everyone except Abel and me canceled at the last minute. I, for one, had no intention of changing my plans so I went ahead and called Abel and said, "It looks like it's just you and me."

That night we wound up driving to Hollywood, walking down Sunset Strip, and having a great time laughing and talking. Abel and I went into Ripley's Believe It or Not! and had a good time except when we came to the exhibit about death—reading about all sorts of weird ways in which people have died didn't sit well with me. Right away Abel noticed I was uncomfortable so he grabbed my hand and took me to another room filled with life and light. Little did I know that later he would do that to my heart. It was one of those evenings where everything is so effortless and fun that time flies by and before you know it, it's time to go home. When I dropped him off at his home that night, Abel commented, "Well, our little date is over. Now back to reality."

What he said really stuck with me, because whether I was ready to acknowledge it or not, deep down inside I was thinking the same thing. And I liked the idea that in his mind it had been a date. For the next few weeks, every time I was around him, I found myself getting butterflies, but I quickly reminded myself, *Oh, no, not Abel—he's just a friend.*

Yet as time went by, I found that no matter how hard I tried, I couldn't shake those butterflies; in fact, I couldn't really stop thinking about him whether we were in the same room or not. I looked forward to seeing him at church every week and whenever we planned one of our group outings, I'd find myself worrying about how I looked, what I was going to wear . . . all because I was thinking about Abel. I fought my own feelings for a long time until I realized that they weren't going anywhere and I had to acknowledge to myself what was going on. I was falling for Abel. So instead of continuing the battle against my own heart, I decided to be honest and let him know what I was feeling, so I plucked up the courage and made my first move by texting him the words, "Hey, I think I like you."

I sent the message because I was almost certain that he didn't like me and I knew he was the type of guy who would be honest and tell me the truth. As soon as he said he didn't like me, I would be disappointed, of course, but at least I could move on and stop wasting time thinking about him.

So I was bracing myself for a rejection when almost right away he texted me back saying: "I like you too."

Big sigh of relief. He liked me back! But also . . . Oh no, now what?

Abel and I started dating soon thereafter and right from the start we got along incredibly well. Abel is a very gentle and loving man, he is wise beyond his years, and there's something about him that always makes you feel at home and safe. And coming from my roller coaster of a love life, being around Abel was healing in ways I could have never imagined; it was the first time I was in a relationship where I actually felt good about myself. And not just from time to time. He made me feel good all the time. He was funny and loving and whenever we were together, I felt happy and cared for. And not only that, I really really liked him. How could I not? He was a hopeless romantic, serenading me at my window at four a.m., but also praying for me when I needed it most. He led me closer to God, which is what my spirit and soul needed most at the time. He was merciful like Jesus and told me my past was gone. He didn't see it and he didn't even want to know about it. To him, I was a new creation. He was a man who accepted me for who I am and that's when I knew I wanted to marry him.

I am ten years older than Abel and while in the beginning that was a huge problem for me, Abel never saw it as an obstacle. He knew he loved me and ultimately through his perseverance, love for the Lord, and his maturity, he won me over within a year. But our families had a different opinion. They didn't accept our relationship at all, and they hoped it was a passing fad; something we would soon get over. Our mother didn't like the situation one bit and even my sister was skeptical.

"So . . . there's this guy at church, Sister," I told Chay one day when I had just started dating Abel. "I think I like him."

Chay was in the middle of recording one of her music videos so I was telling her during one of her breaks.

"Really?" she asked excitedly. She knew how badly I wanted to meet someone. "Do I know him?"

"Yes, Sister," I answered. "You do, it's Abel."

She paused for a moment, squinting her eyes as she tried to put a face to a name.

"Abel? You mean Pete's friend? The guy from church?"

"Yes, Sister. Abel Flores," I answered. "He's on the worship team."

"Oh, Sister, don't be f***ing ridiculous," she answered immediately in a half-laughing, curious, even sympathetic way.

"Sister, for real? Is this what you're going to say to me?"

"Really, Sister. I really like him."

"Oh, don't worry, Sister," she said. "It'll pass, it will pass!"

"No, Sister! I don't want it to pass!" I objected. "I mean it! I like him!"

"Sister . . . really. . . . don't worry about it! You'll get over it."

"But why, Sister, why don't you like him?" I asked.

"It's not that I don't like him, Sister—it's that he's too young."

"What do you mean he's too young?"

"Exactly. He's ten years younger than you," she said.

"So?" I answered quizzically. "What about you and Ferny?"

"Oh, me and Ferny, that's different. We're older."

It wasn't any different, and she knew it! Ferny was ten years younger than she was and she adored him. For a long time, she didn't actually believe me when I said I liked Abel and she dismissed it as a worship team infatuation. But as things became more serious between us, Chay started to worry. She liked Abel and she was of course happy that I had found someone to love and who loved me, but the age difference was something she wasn't able to shake. Even though Ferny was the love of her life, she eventually broke up with him and ultimately considered that the age difference was one of their many problems. She'd say to me that all relationships go through difficult moments and the age difference would just make those trying times and situations that much more challenging. And while I understood that my sister was just looking out for me, I knew that in the case of Abel and me, she was wrong. There was something powerful between us that transcended age.

Our courtship lasted for three years—a record for me, since I hadn't ever really been in a long-term relationship. What was wonderful about being with Abel was that he already knew everything about me and I didn't have to explain. He loves me for who I am—with him I've never had to pretend. I've never had to try to be someone I'm not. All I have to do is be myself and it feels great.

From the moment we started dating, I very clearly told Abel about my sexual abstinence. Since the day of my turnaround, I had vowed not to have sex until I was married and I intended to keep it that way. In my mind, the moment I reconnected with God, I had been born again and my past had been wiped clean. I fully believed that I was the "new creature" the Bible talks about, and I wanted to save myself for my future husband. Abel understood and he was in full agreement with me. He too was saving himself for marriage.

But just when you think you have everything under control, life throws you a curveball. Sometime into our relationship and despite our best intentions, Abel and I fell into sexual sin. One thing led to another and even though it was beautiful and meaningful for both of us, we broke our promise. We felt terrible and we didn't know what to do. In the beginning, we tried to keep it a secret. No one would have had to find out if it hadn't been for the fact that Pastor Pete eventually suspected something was going on and he asked me up front. Now, I may be many things, but there's one thing I'm not, and that's a liar. I simply hate to lie. I'm actually terrible at it; you can see right through me. And whenever I try, I end up confessing two seconds later. So when Pete asked me whether I had had sex with Abel, I had no other choice but to say the truth! I hated being in sin. I felt like a liar and a hypocrite so I was somewhat relieved to have it out in the open. It was like a rescue mission from God before I lost my relationship with Him.

Pete couldn't believe it when I told him. He brought his hands to his head and exclaimed, "Sister! But why did you tell me?"

"Why did you ask?" I answered. I was ashamed of what I had done, but I certainly wasn't going to lie about it!

"Arghhh, Rosie! I asked out of protocol the way I ask all the dating couples at church, expecting them to say no," he answered. "Now what are we going to do?"

I was so embarrassed. And to have to tell my big brother of all people! Eventually, the entire congregation found out and I was in deep trouble: not only had I broken my vow; I had grossly disrespected everyone around us and I felt terrible. It was strange to think of how just a few years earlier I wouldn't have cared the least about what was going on, but now the thought of what I had done was keeping me up at night. I felt as if my world was crumbling. And whenever my world started to crumble, there was one person I knew I could always call. My sister.

"Sister, I'm in huge trouble with the congregation," I started to explain, a grave tone in my voice.

"It's okay, Sister. You're gonna be okay . . . don't worry," she said calmly.

"Sister, I worry I'm not going to be okay; we're talking about the whole congregation. That's about two hundred people!" I said. She patiently heard me out as I told her the whole story.

"Well, Sister, we're kind of in the same mess," she said when I had finished. "But you're in trouble with two hundred people and I'm in trouble with . . . I would say . . . two million."

"What?" I asked in disbelief.

"Yeah, so do you remember that guy I really liked? The one who's like twenty years younger than me?"

"Yes, of course I remember. The guy from your banda."

"Yeah, exactly. That one," she said. "Well, I just found out that someone leaked a video of me pleasuring him."

"Are you serious?" I said, almost falling off my chair.

"Yes, Sister . . . Yet again, it seems like somehow we're connected. So something tells me we're gonna be okay."

Chay was acting strong but I could tell that inside she was devastated. I started crying for her and for myself. How could anyone do this to my sister?

"Oh, Sister, what are you going to do?" I sobbed.

"I don't know, Sister," she answered. "What *should* I do?"

It was amazing to me that my sister was asking me for advice. Here was the strongest woman in the world asking *me* for advice. After everything she had done for me, it made me feel so good to be able to help her, for a change.

"Sister, I think the truth is always best," I said. "Plenty of people film themselves with their partners; there's nothing weird about that," I added. *"He's* the jerk for leaking it!"

The next day, the sex tape scandal erupted and she was getting a lot of heat on the Internet and via social media. It was so infuriating to see people judge my sister for something private that had happened between two people. She was clearly hurting, so I went to see her at one of her events. She was staying in a hotel and I went up to the room to be with her for a while before the concert, not quite sure of what her state of mind would be. She opened the door with a big smile and gave me a huge hug. She was happy to see me, I could tell. I later found out that she had been crying in the closet, but I didn't know it at the time. All I saw was my beautiful, strong, brilliant big sister, smiling and in control of the situation. *She's good,* I said to myself. *My sister is always good.*

We hung out for a while, lying in bed together, just talking. Those memories are priceless, especially now. We'd laugh, we'd cry . . . I'd even watch her sleep peacefully. I loved to see her rest.

Suddenly Chay said:

"So, do you want to see it?"

"Do I want to see what?" I asked.

"The video!"

"No, Sister!" I said. "Are you crazy? I don't want to see it!"

"Oh, come on, just watch it," she said.

"Please no, Sister, no! I don't want to see it!" I said, cracking up as she shoved her phone in front of my face to make me watch it.

"Yes, Sister, you have to watch it!" she said. "If you're going to learn how to do it, you might as well learn from the best. You see, I'm very good in that area, Sister, so watch and learn! Come to think of it, I'm going to become a teacher. I'm going to become a teacher and you should go ahead and learn from me, Sister. Because you know why men cheat on women, right?" she asked.

I rolled my eyes. My whole life, she had been telling me this.

"Because they don't know how to pleasure their men," I answered. And we both cracked up laughing.

That was Chay. No matter how afraid she was, no matter how much pain she was in, courage and laughter always overcame. I'll always love her for that.

In March 2011, Abel proposed. He did it on a beautiful evening he orchestrated himself. He invited me out for a date, and when he came to pick me up he blindfolded me and drove me to a dock by the ocean at Manhattan Beach. I was so nervous I didn't know what was going on! Suddenly he asked me to take my blindfold off and as soon as I opened my eyes I saw him kneeling in front of me and my entire family was standing behind him. Lupillo wasn't there because he was on the road somewhere, but he was aware of the proposal because even though I didn't know it at the time, Abel had already called them all, one by one, to ask for my hand in marriage. He knew how important they all are to me so he made sure he had their blessings.

Abel proposed to me in front of my family because he knew they were the most important people in my life, and he proposed in front of the water because he knew that's what I love the most. Everyone was there and it was a beautiful, touching moment. Even my sister was able to take time out of her crazy schedule to be there. No matter what was going on in her life—and believe me, there was always *a lot* going on—somehow she was there for the people she loved.

I was so nervous that to this day I don't remember what he said exactly, but as soon as he stopped talking I understood it was the moment where I was supposed to say "Yes." Tears started rolling down my cheeks, then suddenly I heard my brother Juan yell out: "Hey, I can't hear anything—what did she say?"

"Can't you see she said yes and they're kissing, stupid?" answered my sister. And we all broke into a huge, boisterous laugh. It was such an emotional moment. Immediately, I got on the phone to tell Lupe. He was so happy for me—he thought Abel was the right man for me, and his blessing meant the world. Chay hugged me tight and we couldn't stop crying. We had both waited for this moment for so long, and I knew she was as excited as I was. And even though she didn't necessarily approve of our age difference, she came to realize how much I loved Abel. And that's just the way she was. She was going to support me no matter what.

Initially I was thinking we would get married the following year, but Abel wanted us to tie the knot as soon as possible, so that's what we did. The date we chose was July 4, 2011, since July Fourth has always been a special day for me, and what better way to celebrate it than by marrying the man I loved? After so many years of pain and uncertainty, to me it was a dream come true. I felt some nervousness and fear, but no doubt after I asked God to confirm that this relationship was His will. The fact was, for the first time in a long time, I saw a future.

My whole family came together to help us plan the wedding. Even though I had been saving up for it since the day I decided to turn my life to the Lord, Chay offered to pay for everything. She wanted me to save my money to buy our first home. Juan paid for the photographer, Gus gave us the DJ, Chiquis gave me my wedding dress, Jacqie gave me my veil, Chay was my matron of honor, Pastor Pete officiated, and first Lupe, then my mom and dad, walked me down the aisle. As Lupe and I came together to walk down the aisle, he told me to grab his finger—just like when I was in first grade and I was nervous about my first day of school. He knew I was nervous about this wedding and by offering me his finger he wanted me to know that everything was going to be okay.

The celebration took place at the Marriott Hotel at Playa del Rey and that July Fourth was one of those beautiful Southern California summer days. The sky was perfectly blue and everything was so bright and crisp, I knew God was in every detail. The ceremony took place outside on the terrace and as I walked down the aisle, I caught a glimpse of Abel standing by Pastor Pete at the altar. He was wearing a dark gray suit and he looked nervous, but so handsome, and in that instant I knew I was marrying the man that would make me happy because he already did. So there, with God and our families and friends as witnesses, we vowed to love and honor each other until death do us part.

After the ceremony came the party. Like at all Rivera parties, there were speeches but this time Abel and I were the ones giving speeches of love and gratitude to our families. By the end of the night, everyone was in tears. Everyone felt God's love and that was exactly what I wanted.

It was an extraordinary day that far exceeded my dreams—an evening worthy of a princess with fireworks lighting the sky as part of our celebration. The best part was that, even though in recent times there had been some squabbles in our family, all my brothers, Mom, and Dad were in attendance—and peace and harmony was the order of the day. It was one of the happiest days of my life.

Months later, we were at my sister's house in Encino at a party. Most of my brothers were there and we were hanging out and having fun. Chay had hired a banda and there was so much noise and laughter all around, one of those moments when I thank the Lord for being a Rivera. Despite the disagreements we may have, despite the hardships we have been through, we always find a way to come back together and be a family. And when that happens, it's magic. It feels like a warm, soothing embrace and you know that there's no other place in the world where you'd rather be.

That particular night, my brothers and my sister were drinking and Lupe, who's always so much fun when he's drunk, ended up in the fountain. My sister kept asking me to take a shot. "Just one, just one!" she'd beg, but I refused. She insisted for a little while but ultimately understood and left me alone, urging the others to stop pressuring me too. It was such fun and we were all cracking up but as the evening progressed, my brothers, being brothers, started to tease and make fun of Abel. My husband is the sweetest, most gentle man, and while my brothers can also be sweet and gentle, they also have big personalities, and I guess Abel was an easy target. But Abel never grew up around men—he has only a younger brother and sister—so he's not used to the harshness of their words. I had been around them my entire life and I knew it was just teasing for the sake of teasing, but Abel didn't and I could see in his face, in his little heart, that he was being hurt.

"*Ay, ya basta,*" I said to them. "Leave him alone! Stop it!"

Abel remained completely silent while my brothers teased on.

My sister, who was sitting right next to me, must have also noticed the pained look on Abel's face because at one point she looked at him and whispered into my ear: "Sister, he's so beautiful."

And I said, "You think so?"

"I know so," she answered. "He has one of the most beautiful souls and hearts that I have ever seen. Because not only does he put up with you, he puts up with your crazy-ass family."

"Yeah, he does," I said, giggling.

If it's even possible, that day I loved Chay more. Even though in the beginning she had so vehemently opposed my relationship with Abel, she was finally seeing him for the beautiful human being he is, and nothing could have made me happier. Nothing.

Chay eventually became a huge fan of Abel. Abel was always a bit shy in front of her, but she loved his voice and she would always ask him to sing whenever we were together. He'd sing me romantic songs like "Para Una Mujer Bonita" by Pepe Aguilar and Chay and I just loved it. And so did Abel! The fact that a huge singer like my sister loved his voice so much made him incredibly happy.

fourteen

wednesdays

The Bible says, "Leave your father and your mother and become one flesh with your husband" which, in other words, means that when you get married, you leave your parents and siblings behind so your family becomes your spouse, and eventually your children. I had read these words a thousand times and understood their meaning, but the reality of what that meant was much more difficult than what I had imagined.

I was thirty years old and I was leaving my mom's home for the first time in my life. I loved my husband deeply and I knew that he loved me too, but it was difficult for me to leave my family behind. In my mind they were still the most important people in my life and I had a lot of trouble learning to put my husband first. They had always been front and center in my life, and it was something I wasn't able to change overnight. If Lupe or Juan, for example, called me at night to ask me for something, right away I'd be out the door.

Abel would ask me, "Where are you going, baby?"

"Lupe needs me, baby. I'll be back," I'd answer.

"But wait, weren't we going to go out on a date?"

"Yeah, I know, baby, but Lupe needs me, sorry," and I'd be out the door. "My family comes first."

He'd say, "Wait a minute, *I'm* your family. I'm your husband!"

"Yeah, but I've known them for thirty years and I've only known you for three. So they win!"

"Yes, babe, but it's *us* now."

"No, babe, I'm sorry!"

In his family, Abel is the oldest by many years, so the connection he has with his siblings is different. They aren't as close . . . or maybe it's just a Rivera thing—or a Rosie thing! I don't know. It might just be that those early lessons in "family always comes first" and always having to stick by your siblings were so deeply ingrained in my soul that I had trouble making room for anything else. My family had been by my side throughout the darkest times in my life. How was I not going to put them first? After all, all my previous relationships with men ended with them leaving or disappointing me, while I knew for sure that my family never would. Abel was extremely patient with me and he understood where I was coming from, but it was very hard for him to see me put everyone else before him.

That first year of marriage was difficult. It wasn't just the troubles with Abel at home that were affecting me; there was a situation unfolding with my family that I just didn't know how to handle.

A few months earlier I had brought Jacqie to the Lord and she too had turned her life to Him. Nothing makes me happier than seeing someone I love discover God's love and the empowering effect it has on all of our lives. Jacqie and I started to preach and sing together at church and we became very close friends.

But as with any friendship, there came a moment when we had a disagreement. I saw things one way, Jacqie saw things another way, and there was no power in Heaven or on Earth that made us see eye to eye. Chay was caught in between. I tried through every way possible to explain and validate my point of view, but nothing seemed to help. We simply couldn't move past the incident. Jacqie was upset, I was upset, and Chay was very upset. She didn't necessarily know who was right and who was wrong; but the fact of the matter was that she wanted the problem to end. And since I wasn't giving in, she did what she thought she had to do: she took her daughter's side. Today I can say that it's water under the bridge and she was absolutely right to do so, but at the time I was devastated. I knew Chay would always choose her children but I needed her to at least understand my point of view. Slowly we began to drift apart.

I fell into a deep depression that was not like anything I had ever felt. Up until that point, no matter how bad things got, or how much pain I was in, I'd just keep moving forward. In fact, in my family, we say that there's no time for depression, no time to dwell on what's wrong. You have to keep your head up and move forward. Just keep moving forward.

But this time was different. For the first time in my life, my sister and I weren't getting along and just like in the times when Trino had threatened to take her life, I was terrified of losing her. I couldn't conceive of a life without Chay. The sadness started to take over every aspect of my daily routine: I couldn't get up in the morning, I could barely eat, and I would spend entire days crying and praying to God for a way out. God would tell me, time and time again, to let go of my pride, to forgive and move on. Yet while I was able to forgive, letting go of the pain was much harder.

Like in other difficult moments of my life, there was silence all around me. The rest of our family was stuck in the middle and they didn't want to get involved. They were just going to sit this one out. No more loud laughs and speeches, just a deafening silence. Juan isn't one to take sides, especially when it comes to his sisters, but he always stands by what he feels is right, and in this case he agreed with me so his relationship with Chay became somewhat strained. No one knew what to do and we all shed tears as we waited for a solution.

All this was going on when one day I found out that Chay had thrown a huge birthday party for one of her kids and everyone in the family had been there—except me. Because I was having such a hard time, and she didn't want to create a situation that was uncomfortable for her daughter, Chay didn't invite me.

It broke my heart. Never in a million years would I have imagined Chay capable of not inviting me to a family event. It was the last straw, what made me realize that this wasn't a disagreement that was simply going to blow over. She was serious, and if I wanted to be a part of her life, I was going to have to do something about it. I said to myself, *No one is going to take me away from my sister. Never.* I understood that having my sister in my life was more sacred than any quarrel or any obstacle that life might throw my way. My sister was the person I loved most in the world and I wasn't going to let anything come between us. So, I called Chay and said to her "You have my blessing, no matter what you do." I accepted my fault and begged God to help me let it go.

My sister accepted my apology and we were able to get past the incident. With time and God's love, I was able to heal my heart and let go; however I have never forgotten the pain I felt over those six months. Our mighty God has a plan for all of us and everything happens for a reason. It is my firm belief that in allowing me to live through that period of estrangement from my sister, God was preparing me for what was to come.

During that first year of marriage, Abel and I found ourselves thinking about money and budgets, and as anyone, perhaps, who is starting out in life, I prayed to God to help us with what I thought I needed most: money.

"Please God, help me find ten thousand dollars."

"That's too simple," God would answer me.

"Okay, then," I'd say surprised. "Then send me twenty thousand dollars."

"That's still too simple, Rosie, think bigger," He said.

"Okay . . . Then how about two hundred thousand dollars?"

"You still don't get it, Rosie. That's too simple," He said to me. "Why don't you try changing that number from dollars to people you can bring to me in order to transform their lives?"

And then I understood. It wasn't enough for me to ask Him to send me money for my own worldly needs. What I needed was to ask for something bigger than myself, bigger than anything I had imagined until then, and that was what was going to bring me true love and happiness.

Whenever I go somewhere to speak, I always thank God for my wonderful family who has offered me amazing things throughout my entire life. I have been spoiled rotten because of the empire my mom and father built, because of what Lupe and Chay accomplished, and everything they did for us. Anything our parents had was given to us and being the youngest, they gave me anything I wanted. I was able to get all the plastic surgery I wanted. I could buy any car, any bag, any clothes. But the truth was that none of it ever fulfilled me. I was unhappy for most of my youth. It's so easy to sit around dreaming of getting one hundred thousand or two hundred thousand dollars and thinking that once we get that, we'll be happy. As soon as I get that plastic surgery, I'll be happy. As soon as I get married, I'll be happy. As soon as I have three kids—two boys and a girl—I'll be happy. Life is filled with these types of happy moments, of course, but if you're broken inside, if you haven't truly opened your heart to all the beauty and love that there is in the world, you will *never* really be happy. My entire life I had wanted peace and love, and I desperately searched for it everywhere I could and I found it in the place I least expected it: God.

As soon as I understood this, I knew what I had to do. My heart was set on reaching the largest number of people to bring to Him. With God's guidance, I went back and forth for a while, thinking about how many souls I was going to bring to him, until finally a number popped into my mind.

"Two million," I said to Him. "I want to help two million women. Two million sexually abused or battered women. I want to help them heal. I will bring You two million people whose lives You will transform."

With that, my mission was now clear.

If I had stopped to think about it too much, if I hadn't known, in my heart, what God is capable of, the enormity of the task at hand might have overwhelmed me. After all, I was no one at the time, just the Rivera's little sister and while my brothers and sister were filling stadiums and amphitheaters with tens of thousands of people both at home and abroad, the biggest audience I've had was a congregation of about two hundred people at our church. How on Earth was I going to accomplish this dream?

With God by my side, I knew that sooner or later I'd find a way. All I had to do was keep my eyes open and never lose sight of the future ahead.

Once we got through that difficult first year of marriage and were able to smooth all the rough patches, Abel and I decided we were ready to have a baby. With my sister back, my promise to God, and a renewed sense of purpose, I started to feel more in control of my new life with my husband. From the way Abel treated my sweet Kassey as if she were his own, I knew he would be a great father and I couldn't wait to welcome our baby into the world.

In the summer of 2012, we started trying to get pregnant. I've always thought I was super fertile like my sister—it took only one look from a guy for her to get pregnant—but nothing happened. A few months went by and I started to worry. Could something be wrong with me? I'd tell my sister my concerns but she'd always shrug them off, saying, "Ah, you're just not trying hard enough, Sister!"

Then a couple of weeks later I was pregnant. As soon as I saw the plus sign on the test stick, I rushed to tell, not Abel, but my sister! She was traveling so I sent her a text.

"Sister, I have news for you," I wrote.

"I'm about to get on a plane—is it important?"

"Don't worry, I'll tell you later."

"Oh, come on, Sister, tell me."

"No, Sister, it's okay. I'll tell you later!"

"Tell me! Now I want to know!"

"I'm pregnant."

"OMG! See, Sister, I knew your uterus worked!"

"It does, Sister!"

"Okay, I'm getting on a plane but I'm going to start thinking of baby names."

I have no idea why she decided to give herself that task. Maybe because she was always coming up with names for everyone and she thought it was a talent that came quite naturally to her. It was all good with me! I was just thrilled at the thought of new life inside me. Later on that same day, she called me, and she already had a list.

"Sister, I'm so happy for you! I have a few names. We can talk about them if you want."

"Sister! I haven't even told Abel yet. Can you please wait for me to tell him?"

"Oh, yes, of course, Sister," she said, pretending to be preoccupied. "But here's what I've been thinking—how about Pharrell?"

"Sister!!!"

"Okay, what do you think of Ice Cube? Or Fo-Real?" she suggested, cracking up. "I mean, you have to be prepared because you're going to have a dark boy."

She said this because Abel's skin tone is darker than mine.

"I know, Sister! I want a dark boy! I love dark boys!"

"I'm just sayin' . . ."

I decided I wanted to surprise Abel with the news on his birthday, which is November 13. So I wrapped the pregnancy test up in a beautiful gift box (gross, I know) and that's what I was going to give him. Chay was going to be there too, so I begged her, "Please Sister, please act surprised. I don't want Abel to know I told you first!"

"Oh, of course, Sister, don't worry, I've got this."

So once Abel's celebration was well under way and all of our families and friends were there with us, I pulled out a wooden domino box and gave it to him. It was a beautiful moment—one that I'll never forget. As soon as Abel opened the box and understood what his gift was, tears started rolling down his face. He was excited and nervous and ecstatic, all at the same time. Seeing him cry made me cry too (I'm sure the hormones did their part) and before long, everyone was hugging and crying and congratulating us—even Chay who, despite her best efforts, went completely overboard in trying to act surprised and ended up looking totally fake. Because I can't lie, later that night I just had to tell Abel the truth but he didn't even care. He was so excited and understood the deep relationship Chay and I had.

When I first came to the Lord, no one had to tell me to stop drinking, smoking, swearing, or clubbing. I made that decision on my own and God broke the chains of addiction. I knew what I had to do and I did it. But the thing was, the only person I was really drinking and smoking and clubbing with at that point in my life was my sister. Whenever she'd go on tour, I'd come along with her and that's when we would go wild and party. Her concerts were always such a blast, and I loved coming along with her. However, giving up partying wasn't a huge sacrifice given the immensity of God's love. His love was more than any earthly temptation. What was hard, however, was giving up spending time with my sister. I didn't miss the drinking. I didn't miss the clubbing; I missed hanging out with my sister. She'd say, "Come on, Sister, let's go out! Why don't you come to this concert with me? Come with me to Mexico! Come on! We'll have so much fun!"

But I would say, "I can't, Sister. I really can't."

"But why?" she'd ask.

"I'm not strong enough yet, Sister. I'll have too much temptation to drink, you know, and smoke, and the boys, and stuff . . ."

She always wanted me to come with her, yet she understood
my reasons and therefore respected my wishes. I loved her so much
for supporting me, but at the same time I was heartbroken that I
couldn't see her as often anymore. With all her travel, coupled
with her other business and family obligations, I rarely got the
chance to hang out with her, lying in bed and talking for hours. I
felt fulfilled and at peace with my new commitment to God but
during that first year I'd cry because I missed her so much. Not
seeing my sister was in fact my biggest sacrifice to God. I didn't
feel anything else was a sacrifice. I felt as if I had to hold back from
going out with my sister not because she was a bad influence,
but because I knew I wasn't strong enough yet. I'd say to God,
"I'm going to sacrifice this, but I beg You, in the same way You've
allowed us to travel the world having fun at concerts, please let
us work together for You. Maybe she can sing and I can preach.
Maybe she can preach and I can sing . . . Allow us God, please, to
work for You."

As much as I was hurting, the thought of the two of us working
for God became my solace, my focus, and my inspiration. I
dreamed of her turning her life around and becoming a believer
and instead of singing she was going to start preaching or doing
evangelical events.

I could see it was already in her—at her concerts sometimes she
would say, "Yeah, right now you guys are all drinking here, but
one day you will be praying here with me."

One of the things that I learned in my Bible studies is that
everything you declare with your mouth comes true and if anyone
was prophetic in the simplest form, it was Chay. As soon as she

said something, it happened, whether it was her life or someone else's. So I began to think, "Okay, God, this is how we're going to get to save those two million souls. My sister is going to sing Christian music and I'm going to preach, right? We're going to do this together."

I dreamed of the two of us traveling the world together, doing events and bringing one, two, twenty million souls to God.

In October 2011, my sister called with a proposal.

"Sister, I want you to do a radio show with me."

"What?" I answered. "How am *I* going to be on a radio show?"

"Come on, Sister! It will be fun!"

"But who's going to like me?" I asked. I understood people wanting to hear Chay on the radio, but why in the world would they want to listen to me?

"Just be yourself, Sister! People are going to love you! All I need is you."

"Okay, but what am I going to talk about?"

"I want you to talk about God. I'm going to give you the last five minutes of the show to talk about God because I love the way you do it. I love the way you don't shove it down people's throats, you don't scare anyone by talking about Hell, you just tell them He loves them. And that's what I want. Do you think you can do that, Sister?" she asked.

I thought about how much I had missed my sister over the past few years and how this would be an opportunity to see her every week, without fail.

"Yes!" I said.

The format was exactly what Chay had said. For the first part of the show, Chay and I would just talk the way we would normally talk and respond to listeners' questions. Then at the last five minutes, I would end on an inspirational note.

The show was called *Contacto Directo con Jenni Rivera* and it was on live, every Wednesday. Soon, Wednesday became my favorite day of the week because I got to see my sister. After those years of not being able to spend as much time with her on the road and partying, it felt like such a relief to have her to myself— albeit in front of a huge radio audience—for four hours each week.

During commercial breaks on the show, Chay and I started dreaming of making a difference in the world on a much larger scale. We talked about one day traveling the globe and filling arenas with a message of hope—where the singing would be secondary to changing lives.

The topic surfaced every couple of weeks and I would remind Chay, "God didn't make you famous just for fun. There's a purpose behind it all."

The next month, in one of the last conversations we had together on the subject, Jenni told me, "Sister, I know we talked about flying to other countries singing and speaking, but I'm really tired. I'll leave the traveling to you, but I wouldn't mind having a weekly event at the Staples Center here in LA."

I laughed. "You really think big, don't you!" We both agreed to pray about the possibilities.

Contacto Directo con Jenni Rivera lasted for exactly fourteen months—from October 2011 to December 9, 2012, and not a day goes by when I don't thank God for giving me that opportunity. Thanks to that radio show, I was able to talk to my sister and see her every week, and I felt like the most blessed person in the world.

Toward the end of November 2012, Chay phoned me and said, "I'd like to come to the Thursday night service with you."

At our brother's church, following a deeply moving meeting, she recommitted her life to the Lord.

Only God knew what would take place a few days later in the mountains of Mexico.

fifteen

the unthinkable

On December 8, 2012, my husband, Abel, and I were attending my niece Karina's wedding in Las Vegas. Most of our family had made it out for the celebration. Only Chay couldn't be there because she had booked a performance in Monterrey, which she simply couldn't cancel—tickets had been booked months in advance and she was never one to cancel on her fans.

As always, Chay and I spent the day texting back and forth. We were *always* texting back and forth—it was one big, never-ending conversation—and that day was no exception. Soon enough—or should I say, as usual—the topic turned to boys. Her divorce was not yet final and she was still pretty torn up about it so I was trying get her mind off her ex-husband by asking her to change her avatar picture on BlackBerry Messenger to one of her and Beto Cuevas, one of her cohosts on *La Voz México.* She was going through a series of avatars featuring her colleagues and friends and I kept teasing her that I wanted one of her and "my new brother-in-law," as I called Beto.

"Go take another picture with him and flirt a little," I texted her.

"Are you crazy? He's just my friend!" she answered.

I believed her and I knew they would never date but I just wanted her to know she was beautiful and strong and she could get any man she wanted. It was a funny, lighthearted conversation, like the thousands of others we'd had throughout our lives. But we never finished it because a few hours later, my cell phone died. I laughed out loud because when this happened, Chay would always complain to me: "Sister, that's so irresponsible! Carry a charger with you." She was right, of course. Today, I make sure to carry my charger because a "dead" cell phone always reminds me of my sister, and how I can't allow it to happen. But right then I didn't give it much thought. *Oh well, I'll catch up with her tomorrow when we're back home.*

The wedding took place at The Little White Chapel in Vegas and it was a simple but beautiful ceremony. With almost every Rivera in attendance, it was a loud and boisterous affair before the ceremony but once it began, we were all smiles and tears. Karina looked beautiful and we were all so glad to see her happy. Gus was the proudest dad you've ever seen and it was great to see him so happy as well. After the ceremony, we all went to a huge buffet at a fancy hotel and made a ruckus—the party almost ended with the traditional Rivera cake fight but we ultimately decided to spare the bride and not get kicked out of the hotel the way we had been kicked out of Chuck E. Cheese—twice.

Abel and I had an amazing time but instead of staying in Vegas that night, we decided to drive back home to Los Angeles after the reception. We got in the car at around one a.m. and settled in for the four-hour drive. Abel and I drove back with Kassey and Jacqie, her husband and her daughter. I was exhausted and normally I would have fallen asleep right away, but something inside me felt off. There was this uneasiness in the car. Everyone was asleep except Jacqie and me. I had just spanked Kassey and I was feeling so bad because I never spank Kassey—she is just about the sweetest, most loving child in the entire world—so I woke her up and said, "*Hija*, come here, I'm sorry I spanked you. I stand firm that you shouldn't have done what you did, but I shouldn't have spanked you. Do you want to talk about it?"

"It's okay *Mami*, don't worry about it, I understand," she answered gently, her eyes still heavy with sleep. "I shouldn't have been acting like that."

"Okay, baby, I love you," I answered, and gave her a kiss as she dozed off again.

I turned back around, hoping that now I'd be able to fall asleep, but nothing. I felt a strange tightness in the pit of my stomach and I just couldn't relax. I turned around to look at Jacqie and noticed she, too, was still wide awake.

"You can't sleep?"

"No, *Tía*, I can't," she answered.

I said, "Yeah, me either, Mama."

Jacqie told her husband she missed her mom and even though I didn't say a word, in my heart I couldn't agree more. How I missed the days before she became famous.

The rest of the way we drove in absolute silence, the highway lights flashing by.

When we finally got home a few hours later, I was tired and all I wanted was to get some rest. I don't know what time I ended up dozing off, but I do know that when the phone started ringing at around seven a.m., I immediately regretted not having turned it off. Who in the world could be calling this early in the morning? I saw the cell phone screen flashing on my nightstand, but could barely open my eyes so I just let it ring. I was too exhausted. I remember thinking it was probably just my brother Lupe. Sometimes, when he has too much to drink, he drunk dials me and serenades me with a beautiful song. When he does it, I actually don't want to pick up so I can record it! A call at seven a.m. on a Sunday probably meant he had been out late so I figured I'd just let it go to voice mail in case I was in for a special treat.

But just a few seconds later, the cell phone started ringing again. I tried to ignore it, but then I got a strange feeling. What if it was something important? I stumbled over to my nightstand and grabbed the phone. Sure enough, it was Lupe.

"Rosa?" he asked.

"Yes, Brother . . ." I answered groggily.

"I need you to stay calm. No matter what happens, promise me you will stay calm."

My stomach tightened.

"Okay," I said, "I promise."

Lupe paused for what felt like an eternity.

"Janney's plane is missing," he said finally.

"What?"

"They just called me from Mexico. Her plane is missing. We're doing everything we can to find it."

I'm not sure I was really able to process what he was saying at that moment, but my mind decided to focus on the word "missing." If the plane was missing, that meant it could be found, so I was going to think only about that. Surely, Chay couldn't be *gone*. She was clearly *missing*, so she was going to be found.

"Rosa, I need you to take care of Mom. It's all over the news at this point so please go over there as soon as you can and don't let her watch TV or go on any social media. Just keep her busy until we know more. Pete is already on his way over."

"Okay, Brother," I mumbled, too stunned to say anything else.

I hung up the phone, and thought, *I'm gonna stay calm. I promised Lupe, I'm gonna stay calm.* I remember I didn't even pray to God at that moment. I usually speak to Him about everything, but at that moment I didn't reach out to Him because I was too afraid to hear Him tell me that she wasn't going to be found. I just assumed she was going to be found. She had to be. The idea that something had happened to my sister wasn't even in the realm of possibility. Like a zombie, I glanced at the cell phone screen in front of me and finally pulled up my Twitter account in order to confirm what Lupe had just told me. Sure enough, people were already tweeting: *It's so sad that she is gone. Rosie, you have our condolences.*

I was furious. Who did they think they were, sending me condolences? Immediately, I shot back:

Don't you dare offer me condolences. You don't know that she's gone yet.

At the time, Abel and I were living at my mother's house. After my depression I had decided to quit my great job at Infinity to begin writing my book. I needed to find a stronger sense of purpose and for years, I had been wanting to write about my experience of sexual abuse. I finally felt it was time. It was a huge risk, but Chay had my back and she was so proud of what I was doing. But just a month after I quit my job, Abel was laid off from his job in quality control so we started to have money issues and Mom kindly took us in to live with her until we were able to get back on our feet.

That morning, I went out to help my mom prepare breakfast,

trying to act as normal as possible. But a few minutes later, when Pastor walked through the door, she immediately knew something was up since on Sunday mornings he is usually busy preparing for service.

"What are you doing here?" she asked when she saw me and Pete. "It's early. Aren't you going to go to church today?"

"No, Mom, I think we're just going to hang out here today," Pete said, taking the lead. "We're always busy on Sundays. I just want to hang out with you. I want to take you out to breakfast. Let's spend some time together!"

"Why?" she asked, completely surprised.

I could barely hold back my tears. The thought of Chay missing, coupled with the sight of my mother, still unaware of what was going on, broke me down inside. I felt as if any minute I could break down, but I knew I had to stay strong for the sake of my mother. Yet no matter how much Pete and I tried to act casual, my mama is a smart lady and she knew something was going on. What surprised her the most was that Pete was there—he is the pastor of our church and it made no sense that he should be paying her a spontaneous visit on a Sunday morning.

We did our best to field her questions and keep her occupied, while running back and forth to a room where we had a television on quietly. All the stations were reporting, "Jenni Rivera's plane has gone missing in the mountains of Northern Mexico." Soon, the breaking news was: "The plane of recording superstar Jenni Rivera has been found. Every section of the private jet is broken and there are no survivors."

My mind went into overdrive with every possible scenario. Something had to have happened that we simply weren't aware of. Perhaps she had decided not to get on that plane at the last

minute. Or maybe someone had kidnapped her and they were going to call us for money. Maybe she was being held against her will
and was fighting to get back to us. Maybe . . . just maybe. My
mind was overflowing with maybes as I tried to grasp onto anything that allowed me to believe that Chay was still alive.

A few minutes later, I was on the phone with someone when
suddenly I heard my mother let out a bloodcurdling scream. We
had left her alone for a moment when the phone rang in the other
room. My mother picked up and a distraught fan immediately
asked her: "Is it true that Jenni is gone? That she died in a plane
crash?"

"*That's* why you're here!" she yelled. "You didn't tell me anything!" She went straight for the TV. Her eyes were filled with pain
and disbelief and all she could utter was the question: "Why didn't
you tell me?"

Pete and I tried to explain.

"Mom, we wanted to make sure it was true. You know how
people make stuff up . . . and we didn't want to upset you. We're
sorry, but with your health problems, we have to take care of you."
But she was hearing none of it. From that moment on she was
glued to the television, going back and forth between stations to
watch the latest reports, waiting, hoping, for someone to announce
that Chay had been found and that she was alive and well.

But as we all now know, that news never came. With every
passing minute, Chay's disappearance became more and more real
even though our hearts and our minds didn't want to believe it. In
the following hours, slowly but surely, the rest of the family started
to arrive at the house—my brothers, their spouses and their children, Chiquis, the rest of Chay's children and even my father. Even
though Mom and Dad barely spoke to each other at the time, he

joined us as soon as he heard the news. Every family has its problems and ours is no exception, but one thing is true and that is we are always there for one another when things get tough.

Every Spanish station carried the story nonstop. A number of us decided not to watch TV because many of the things they were reporting were pure speculation and had not been confirmed. But in those first hours, this is more or less what we did know: on the night of Saturday, December eighth, Jenni performed to a sold-out crowd at the seventeen-thousand-seat indoor arena in Monterrey, Mexico. The show ended at around two a.m., December ninth, and, after a local press conference, she, along with publicist Arturo Rivera, attorney Mario Macías, makeup artist Jacob Yebale, and hairstylist Jorge "Gigi" Sánchez, boarded a Learjet piloted by Miguel Pérez and Alejandro Torres, heading to Toluca, where she was to appear on *La Voz México*. The plane took off at three fifteen a.m. from Monterrey and about sixty miles into the flight due to causes yet to be determined by the authorities, it fell twenty-eight thousand feet and crashed into the mountains of Nuevo León, smashing to the ground at about six hundred miles an hour.

All sorts of rumors started to surface. People said that the plane, built in 1969, was not properly maintained; that the sixty-seven-year-old pilot wasn't supposed to fly at night because of his bad vision; that it was all a conspiracy. In times of pain, as humans, we struggle to find explanations for what seems impossible to comprehend. The accident was so absurd; to me it simply couldn't be true.

I was a complete mess, but trying so hard to hold it together for the sake of my mother, for the sake of my father—for the sake of Chay's children, especially. By then, pretty much every member of our immediate family had showed up, and there were about forty of us, all under one roof. The house felt so crowded, but at the same time we were one another's comfort, and the little solace we found was in one another's arms. Some of us were preparing food; others were cleaning or doing anything to keep busy and not have to think. Our brothers and I were looking for flights to go and search for her. All of us wanted to go look for her in the hills. We needed to get her back.

I felt torn between the realization of what had happened, and the hope I still held, deep in my heart, that somehow Chay had survived. Just the day before the accident, she and I had been texting back and forth, making jokes and laughing like we usually did. How could she possibly be *gone*? How could she be so present one moment and so absent the next? I would text her and send BBM messages and she wouldn't answer. *Chay always replies. This can't be it,* I said to myself over and over again. *She can't have been on that plane.*

Chay's kids were going through the same thing, or even worse. They were hearing the reports, but they didn't want to believe what they were saying. There was still no official confirmation that Chay had been on that plane and we were all holding on to that glimmer of hope. I wanted to protect Chay's children from all the crazy reports we were seeing, but I also needed to be honest with them.

"*Tía*, if she's gone, you have to tell us," they said to me.

"If you can handle it, I will tell you," I promised.

Shortly thereafter, they found a picture of her foot on the Internet and they asked me, "*Tía*, is that her foot?"

I didn't tell them she was gone but I answered, "It could be that they cut it off and they're trying to let us know that she's kidnapped, but yes, that's her foot." In such times of crisis, your mind can take you on a wild ride. With childlike faith, we were all hoping against hope but the moment they asked me, I told them what I knew. I had to.

Hours went by and I could feel my soul shattering into a million pieces. With every ticking minute, I came closer to the realization that Chay might never come back. But I still couldn't bring myself to talk to God. I needed Him so badly, but I couldn't speak to Him. To me, not talking to God is like not talking to my best friend or my husband. It was as if I was telling Him not to talk to me if He was going to tell me something I didn't want to hear. I simply wasn't ready to hear it from Him because hearing it from Him meant that my worst nightmare had come true.

But I kept thinking, what can I do? All I knew how to do when I had a problem at this point in my life was worship Him. I was in the choir, I was on the worship team, and worshipping God was what I had learned to do whenever I needed to get through a storm, whenever I felt lost and alone. So even though I wasn't able to speak directly to God, I reached out to the worship team from church and asked them to join me in worshipping our Lord. They came over right away and as the sun set on that first night without my sister in the world, we gathered in my mother's living room and quietly sang His glory.

From the moment the first news reports started to surface, a steady stream of people began to congregate in front of Mom's house. They were Chay's fans, wanting to offer us their support in our darkest hour. They brought flowers, food, and water to share with us and among themselves, paper butterflies, bottles of tequila, and heartwarming cards of sympathy, letting us know how much she and her music meant to them. She had given them so much; now they were there to give her and her family all their love and support in return.

At one point, we looked out the window and noticed that the group of fans congregated on the front lawn had swelled to a crowd of about four or five hundred people. It was beautiful and completely overwhelming. To see so many people we didn't even know standing there, crying and praying for our sister as if she were a member of their families, gave me a feeling I will never be able to describe. So I said to Abel and our friends from church, "Let's go out there and help them through this time of pain." I don't know how I summoned the strength to say that because at this moment of grief, I thought I was going to lose my mind. "Let's go outside," I repeated. In the front yard, with the large crowd gathered, we sang and worshipped, and, with a broken heart, I told them, "I don't know if my sister is on Earth or in Heaven, but whatever happens in life, there is always hope." Then I added, "This one thing I do know: I will see my sister again."

I told them that we were going through a really difficult time, but God was holding us up—and whatever pain they faced, there is a higher power waiting to give them strength. "Thank you for loving us," I continued. "Keep praying. No matter what happens, we're going to be okay. God loves us and He loves YOU."

The next day, December tenth, we began to make plans to bring our sister back from Mexico. Whether she was dead or alive, we had to bring her back. Lupe was on his way back from another town in Mexico where he had been performing, and we were just waiting for him to get home to Long Beach so we could all set out together. The thought of Chay being all alone on that mountain was unbearable. Chiquis and Mom would stay home with the kids while Gus, Pete, Lupe, Juan, and I flew out to Nuevo León to bring her back.

We were in the middle of making all the arrangements when I got a call from Chay's attorneys asking me to meet with them as soon as possible.

"We need you to come in," they said on the phone. "There are some things we need to tell you that are absolutely necessary."

That's when I remembered Chay had asked me to be her trustee. Did that call mean that the day had come?

Abel and my sister-in-law Mona drove me to the attorney's office and I'll never forget that on the way there, a Christian song by Jesus Culture came on the radio and it said, *Giver of each breath, walk with me. Healer of my soul, walk with me.* I knew exactly where I was going—I was going to see her trust attorneys, whose names I knew by heart but I had never met. Chay had always kept her businesses in the hands of her businesspeople so I could just be her sister. But the fact that these two worlds were colliding meant something terrible had happened. So I sang that song and I asked God, "Just walk with me, I'll go wherever You want, wherever it is this journey is going to take us, but please, just don't leave me alone, walk with me. Whatever You have prepared, just walk with me." I was trying not to pray because I still didn't want to talk to Him, but that was what I was singing to Him.

When we got to the attorneys' offices in Santa Fe Springs, they sat me down and said:

"We know your sister's plane has gone missing."

"Yes, it's missing," I responded.

"Do you know that she left you as trustee?"

"Yes, I know," I answered very calmly. "She informed me."

"Okay, well, it is our duty to tell you what her will says," they responded.

"With all due respect, her death has not been confirmed yet," I said. "I don't want to know what's in her will because I want to respect her privacy. I don't want to know a thing about her will until it's absolutely one hundred percent confirmed that she's gone. If you need to tell me something now, please, let it be the very bare necessities. I don't want to know anything else."

So they told me. They said I was her trustee, and that absolutely, under no circumstance, was she to be cremated. That was what they needed me to know. But then there was another note. I was going to have to make a lot of decisions so she had a final message for me: "You've got to be strong, Sister. Be very, very strong. It's not time to quit." She said she trusted me and that I knew why she had chosen me and that I wasn't to let anyone influence my decisions, not even our parents or our brothers.

"Okay," I said, choking back the tears, hoping I would never need to follow her instructions.

The ride back home felt like an eternity. Chay's words resonated deeply in my mind: "Be very, very strong. It's not time to quit."

By the time I got back home, my brothers were arguing. They were clearly not agreeing on something. I had been gone for just a couple of hours, but somehow the plan had changed. We were no longer going to Mexico all together. Only Lupe was going to go and they had flipped a coin to decide who was going with him, and it turned out that person was Gus. I hadn't even been included in the raffle because I was a girl.

"What are you talking about?" I exclaimed. "Of course I'm going! She's my sister too!"

"Rosa, you're a girl and you're pregnant," said Lupe.

"But I want to go! She deserves for me to go!" I screamed back.

"No, Bubba, I think you should stay with Mom and the kids," said Juan.

And because it was Juan—the sibling I am closest to next to Chay—I accepted.

But Chiquis was definitely not okay with the arrangement. She wanted Juan to go and she was adamant about it.

"You have to go, *Tío* Juan, because I know you will bring my mama back. You will search for her and you'll bring her back," she said.

I couldn't blame her. Juan had remained by her side during those difficult months leading up to the accident, and he was the *tío* she trusted most. Plus, everyone knows that the most loyal, bighearted person in our family is Juan. Loyalty runs strong in him and if there's someone you can count on to never let you down, it's Juan.

"The kids and I took a vote," Chiquis said. "And we want *Tío* Juan to go too. *Tío*, bring my mama home."

Right before they headed out to the airport, I called a quick family meeting in my mother's bedroom and told them, in the calmest, most humble way possible, what the attorneys had told me that morning:

"Chay *me dejó de albacea,* she left me as her trustee."

They all nodded without saying a word.

"But I want you guys to know that if she was kidnapped, I think we should sell everything to get her back. I don't care what it takes—we'll sell it all."

Everyone agreed without hesitation. It was a beautiful moment because despite all our differences, there were no doubts in anyone's mind that we would all pull together to get Chay back. Our father had taught us well. *Family always comes first.*

"So just remember, when you're over there," I repeated, "do whatever it takes to bring her back, Brothers. Just bring her back."

· · ·

Juan and Gus spent hours and hours on that mountain searching for Chay. They threw themselves, heart and soul, into finding our sister. God only knows what they saw on that mountain but they stood strong and kept their promise.

Back home, minutes felt like hours while we poured over Internet pictures and waited for any scrap of news we could get.

Chay's son Johnny was looking at maps of the area, and he said to me:

"Look, *Tía*, there is a river three miles from where the plane fell, and knowing my mama, she's going to go toward water because she's smart, so tell *Tío* Juan to go look by the river."

We all held hope that she was still alive somewhere, that she was safe, but in our hearts, we all feared the worst.

On December twelfth, my brothers started to identify body parts. The rest of us were still at home so we knew nothing of this, but I received a call from Gus.

"Hey Rose, does Janney have a scar on her back?" he asked.

That was the moment I knew she was gone. When I saw the foot, I still held hope that she was being held for ransom. But when my brother, who would never know if she did, asked me about a big long scar . . . I knew.

"Brother, you're looking at her stomach," I said.

We both stayed silent for a moment.

"All right, thank you, Sister," he said.

"Thank you, Brother," I said and we hung up.

The kids were sitting next to me and they saw new tears rolling down my face.

"Was it about Mama?" Chiquis asked.

"Yes" I said, pausing for a moment, remembering I had promised I would tell them when I knew. "Your *Tío* Gus just asked me about a scar."

"Yeah, that's my mama's scar," said Chiquis, her gaze turned inward.

I didn't have to confirm anything. They knew.

A few hours later, I got another call from Juan. Apparently Lupe and Gus were having an argument because Lupe had just told Gus that he had made a special urn—a red urn that he designed himself—in order for Chay to be cremated. He was asking Gus to sign some papers in order to arrange for the cremation.

Gus was horrified. He was searching for his sister because he wanted to bring her home to Long Beach, yet Lupe was making an urn. He was heartbroken and with tensions running so high, a fight erupted. Juan, who had been watching the two argue, told them they should call me and ask whether I knew anything.

"Rosie, did Chay say anything about being cremated?" he asked me on the phone.

"Yes, Brother," I answered. "She said she absolutely cannot be cremated."

While that put an end to the discussion at hand, it was too late. Something was broken. The incident carved a breach between my two brothers, one that would eventually break out into war. Gus was so hurt that Lupe had already had an urn made for Jenni. In his mind, Gus was still thinking he could find her while Lupe was already making plans for her cremation. Obviously, everyone has their own way of dealing with pain in situations like these and it's impossible to judge—while Gus still wanted to find Chay and bring her home, Lupe was thinking more practically. Lupe wanted to honor her, and preparing for her cremation, taking care of what needed to be done, was his way of doing so.

Meanwhile for me, the moment her death was confirmed, the situation couldn't have become more surreal. I was officially her trustee and as such I was receiving all these phone calls asking for me to make decisions. Since I'm the youngest and probably the most introverted of my siblings, I usually just sit back and watch them do their thing. I'm never, ever the center of attention. They were all calling to ask me for permission to do things—they needed my signature for DNA tests, powers of attorney, authorization forms. It felt so strange. These were the men I had admired all my life. I respected them so much and the fact that they were now calling *me* to ask for permission to do things felt very strange. It was a new paradigm and that was the moment I knew my life had changed.

On December thirteenth, my brothers and Chay finally came home.

Lupe called to let me know that they were going to fly into Long Beach Airport and he asked that only Pete and I come to meet them.

We weren't given an exact time of arrival, so Pete and I were waiting at the airport for hours. Long Beach Airport is pretty small and I had been there once before with my sister when she had gotten a private jet to go on one of her big tours. As I waited for the plane to arrive, I remembered being at that airport with her and how, when we got to the plane, we weren't impressed with the comfortable seats or the five-star service. What really impressed us was that they gave out freshly baked cookies! *Can you believe it, dude? They're freshly baked!*

I could almost hear her voice telling me: "Now, now, Samalia.

Let's just eat half a cookie because you know it all goes straight to your thighs!"

She was always telling me how everything goes straight to the thighs! *God,* I thought. *Was I really never going to hear that voice again?*

When the jet finally arrived, they pulled up to where we were waiting and Lupe came out first.

"Rosa, do you want to come inside the plane?" he asked.

"Yes, I want to see my sister," I said, tears rolling down my face.

"You can't see her, Rosa," he said calmly as he saw me in tears.

"But I want to see her!" I sobbed.

"You can't in this state," Lupe said. "So if I let you on the plane, you need to be really calm. You can't try to open the box. Promise?"

"Okay, Brother. I promise."

Pete went in first, so the four boys were there with her. I can't imagine what Pete and Gus were feeling that day because ever since they were little boys, they had been in charge of protecting Chay.

When my turn came, I got on the plane and there I found my very strong, voluptuous, five-foot-two-thinking-she's-five-foot-nine, beautiful sister . . . in a box. A small box with a burgundy silk cloth.

"This is her?" I asked.

"Yes, Rosie. I promise it's her," Gus said. "I made sure it's her."

I sat there for a while, just trying to process the fact that that box was my sister, that she was really in there. Never again would I see her face, her hair, never again would I feel her warm embrace. A deep sadness washed over me, but it wasn't like the sadness I had been feeling over the past several days. This sadness was raw and violent, and it was burning me up inside. No matter how hard I tried, I couldn't make it stop and all I could think was that I needed just one more hug. I said to God, "Please give me just one more hug. Just one more." I wanted to feel my sister's arms around me. I wanted her to feel me hug her and tell her everything was going to be okay. So I hugged the box as tight as I could and I don't know if she was hugging me because I needed her, or if I was hugging her because over the previous months she had been hurting so much. I wanted her to know she was going to be okay, she was with God now and nothing could hurt her anymore. I was going to be strong and take care of her babies and one day we would all meet again in Heaven.

The hardest part of that day was having to tell our mother. No one had called her yet; all she knew was that my brothers were coming home. When we got to the house she was just sitting on the couch with the kids; they were all huddled together. As soon as we walked through the door, she looked up at Juan, no one else but Juan. Juan looked back at Mom and just gave her a tiny little nod.

And then everyone knew.

They all broke into tears. Since I had already felt it, I thought, *Okay, when they find out, I have to take care of everyone else.* I tried to touch Jenicka's knee but she didn't want to be touched, which was of course totally understandable. Johnny was very upset. My mom was screaming, Dad was very quiet, and Chiquis and the kids held one another and wept. . . . Seeing everyone else's pain, I couldn't cry; I couldn't even move. All I wanted was to make things better for the kids, the way Chay had always made things better for me. Over the course of the next few days, I did everything I could to take care of everyone else. There was so much to do, so many decisions to make, and I was simply going through the motions, doing everything I could to keep myself occupied and not think about the fact that I was never going to hug, kiss, or receive a text message from my sister ever again.

I tried my best to stay calm for my baby. The innocent child Chay had named Fo-Real . . . because like the Riveras, he'd be the real deal. I broke down only once during December (several more would follow in my closet in 2013), the day my friend Gladyz, who had hung out with Chay and me so many nights and was there in all Rivera moments of joy and sadness, came to take care of me. When I saw her, it hit me that I would never hear Chay call me Samalia again and I let out the loudest scream I could. I fell to my knees in the kitchen and Gladyz went down to the floor to hug me and pick me back up as I sobbed uncontrollably in her arms.

My sister was gone.

sixteen

a life-changing celebration

In the six days that followed her return to Long Beach, the entire family came together to plan Chay's funeral, or "Celestial Graduation," as we decided to call it. Chay was always a straight-A student and while life didn't afford her the honor of graduating from a top university, something she always dreamed of, we were going to make sure she graduated from life on this Earth—with honors. Jenni Rivera was an extraordinary human being in every aspect of her life, and we wanted to make sure that was how the world remembered her.

While Chay left us with clear instructions on what to do in the event of her passing, nothing was clearer than "Cuando Muere una Dama" ("When a Lady Dies"), a song she wrote and recorded back in 2003. The beautiful lyrics told us everything we needed to know:

Quiero una ultima parranda,
por allá en mi funeral.
Todos los que me quisieron,
la tendrán que celebrar,
recordando mi sonrisa
y mi forma de llorar.

I want a final party
For my funeral.
All those who loved me
Will have to celebrate.
Remembering my smile,
And the way I cried.

Fui una guerrillera fuerte
que por sus hijos luchó,
recuerden muy bien que en
    vida
su madre no se rajó,
con la frente muy en alto,
despídanla con honor.

I was a strong soldier,
Who fought for her children.
Don't forget that while she was
    alive
She never quit.
So with your head held high,
Say good-bye to me with
    honor.

Quiero mi grupo norteño,
y que sea con tololoche,
échense un trago por mí
y también un que otro toque.
Ya se fue la hija del pueblo,
la mujer de los huevotes.

I want my norteño band
May there be tololoches
Have a drink in my name
And play a few tunes.

(. . .)

(. . .)

A mi familia querida
mis padres y mis hermanos
se muy bien que en la
    otra vida
volveremos a juntarnos para
    reír y gozar
de lo mucho que triunfamos.

My dear family,
My parents and my siblings,
I know very well that in the
    next life,
We're going to meet again.
To laugh and talk of all our
    triumphs.

Y no me extrañen mis jefes que	*Don't miss me, Mom and Dad,*
su hija la rebelde	*Your daughter the rebel will*
por siempre vivirá.	*always live.*
Que en mi lindo Playa Larga	*In my beautiful Long Beach*
haya una última parranda,	*Have one last party,*
que me canten mis hermanos,	*My brothers will sing,*
mi madre flores reparta,	*My mother will give out flowers,*
mi padre fotografías,	*My father will give out photos,*
y mi hermana lea mi carta.	*And my sister will read my letter.*
Tomen tequila y cerveza,	*Drink tequila and beer,*
que toquen fuerte las bandas,	*The band will play loud music,*
suelten por mi mariposas,	*Release butterflies for me,*
apláudanme con sus palmas,	*Clap your hands for me,*
por que así es como celebran,	*For this is how you'll celebrate,*
cuando se muere una dama.	*When a lady dies.*

Chay wrote "Cuando Muere una Dama" when one of her fans, Blacky, passed away before her performance at the Gibson. Chay sang at her funeral and something clicked inside her. It got her thinking about how she wanted to be celebrated when she passed away. Shortly thereafter she wrote the lyrics and showed them to me one day when we were in her car parked in front of her house. She waited patiently while I read, though before I got to the end there were already tears streaming down my face.

"It's beautiful," I said once I finished. "But I never want to hear it."

She was surprised to hear me say that because I was usually a huge Jenni Rivera fan. I'd listen to her songs on repeat for days.

"I never want to see it become a reality," I explained. "I never want to live without you and if you die, I promise I'll throw myself in the coffin with you."

Chay paused and looked at me. She knew exactly what I meant.

"I know, Sister, I know," she answered. And after a brief pause, she added, "But it's still a badass song, right?"

"Right!" I said, breaking into laughter.

I stayed true to my promise and listened to the song only once before hearing it again on December ninth. And to this day, it breaks my heart to listen to it.

We all knew we wanted Chay's Celestial Graduation to be a celebration, a reflection of her life and the beautiful person she was, but that meant different things to each and every one of us. Some wanted an intimate event with only the family; others wanted a big Michael Jackson–type tribute. We all love Chay in our own way and we wanted to honor her in the way that felt best to us. There were some discussions within the family but ultimately we decided to have an event that would include all the important people in Chay's life, her family, her friends, and of course her fans. After her family, Chay lived for her fans and it simply didn't feel right to have an event that didn't include them. So we decided to have the event at the Gibson Amphitheater, the place where my sister had some of her favorite concerts with her L.A. fans. Even though she had grown big enough to fill the Staples Center, she often said the Gibson was her favorite because it felt more intimate and she was closer to her audience. In fact, she had planned to come back to the Gibson in March 2013 in a concert called "Unbreakable."

In the days leading up to the Celestial Graduation, Chay's son, Michael, worked tirelessly to prepare his mother's cocoon, the beautiful wooden box that would hold her remains during the ceremony and in her final resting place. She had specified that she wanted a red cocoon and since we weren't able to find one that was the exact color she wanted, we had a special one made and Juan, Gus, and Michael sanded it down before it could be painted red. I cannot imagine what was going through his mind as he prepared Chay's cocoon but I know it was everything she would have dreamed of for herself—a beautiful red cocoon decorated with seven butterflies—five for her children and two for her grandchildren at the time—to honor our very own "Mariposa del Barrio."

I was struggling to find a place in my new role of trustee while planning every detail of the celebration and at the same time mourning my sister. I spent every day and every night thinking about her, about what she would have wanted, what she might have thought about this or that decision. I was overwhelmed and I realized I was still angry at God because I wouldn't talk to Him in our daily jogs. I didn't understand why He had taken her from me. I hadn't been able to speak to Him since December ninth until one day I couldn't take it any longer. I went out for a jog and cried out to God at the top of my lungs, "I want my sister back! Why did You do this? What happened to our plan? What happened to our two million souls? How in the world do You expect me to do this if not with my sister?" In my pain and desperation, I thought He could hear me if I shouted loud enough.

My sister was part of the dream. We were going to travel the world together and change people's lives; we were going to bring them God's love and show them that they no longer needed to be afraid. But now that Chay was gone, who would care or listen to Rosie without Jenni? How was I going to do God's will without my sister?

I felt as though He was waiting for me to speak up about my

anger and let it out verbally so that I could discover what He already knew, since He knows my deepest thoughts and feelings before I open my mouth to say them or even rationalize them into thoughts. My anger didn't scare Him away or make Him upset. He showed me how it separated me from Him, but He wasn't separating from me. He was waiting, kindly and mercifully, to help me deal with the wide range of emotions I was having now that my greatest fear had come true.

Then I felt God speak to my heart again: "The plan for the two of you to travel the world together was your idea, but I'm still working on you reaching two million people."

I took a deep breath. God was still there. He hadn't forgotten about me, and our plan was still in play. That day I understood that as humans we set our own goals and objectives, and while the Lord hears them, it is ultimately only His will that counts.

On December 19, 2012, the entire Rivera family, along with almost seven thousand of my sister's fans attended her Celestial Graduation at the Gibson Amphitheater, a couple of thousand outside, and many millions more followed the celebration via the live broadcast on Spanish-language television. Together we all sang and cried and laughed, and prayed. We celebrated her life the way she would have wanted it to be celebrated.

Every member of our family was dressed in white, except my mother, who wore red—Chay's favorite color. In the background, on three large screens, were beautiful photos of Chay at many stages of her childhood, family life, and career. We wanted people to see not only Chay the *"Diva de la banda,"* but also Chay the mother, the sister, the daughter. The incredible woman we all loved.

We started the event with the same intro music Chay used at her concerts—a five-minute musical summary of who she was as an artist. Anytime that music started blaring out of the speakers at one of her events, her fans knew it meant she was about to appear onstage and the crowd swelled with excitement. In planning the ceremony, we wanted her fans to feel those same emotions for the last time. Thinking back, I realize maybe we needed to feel those same emotions; maybe we needed to feel that at any moment Chay was going to make her appearance.

On the stage there was nothing but a catwalk (like the ones she had for her concerts), thirty-five chairs for the family, and a microphone under a spotlight, representing her presence. The men in the family—my father, my brothers, and Chay's two sons—and I were backstage with the cocoon in silence. We were praying for strength and peace. We had said to one another that we weren't going to cry—we wanted to remain strong and serene for our beautiful Diva. We were all wearing white gloves because we had the responsibility of carrying the cocoon to its place in the center of the stage.

As soon as the music started, Chay's daughters, along with my mother and the rest of the family, walked onstage to their assigned seats. As the music started to take over the amphitheater, I began to feel butterflies in my stomach, just like the many times before when my sister was about to go onstage. But any excitement I felt was crushed when I realized she was lying in the cocoon next to me and she was never coming back. I was holding back tears, trying to be strong like my brothers but then Lupe began to cry. And I couldn't hold it in anymore. Tears streaked down my face and before long Juan was also crying. We had a few seconds to collect ourselves before our cue came and we started walking forward to give the Diva her grand entrance.

And we did. We carried the Queen to her spot on the catwalk.

Those were the hardest one hundred steps I've ever had to take but the crowd loved it—I could hear them cheer and sob, all at the same time, all for their beloved Jenni. Every single emotion possible was palpable and in that beautiful moment of joy and despair, we shared the heaviness of one another's sorrow.

When we finally arrived at her spot on the stage, we carefully placed the cocoon on its stand and touched it, as if wanting to reassure her by letting her know that we would be right there next to her. I bent down and kissed the cocoon as I would have kissed her on her forehead. I don't know why but in that instant, I saw the strongest woman in the world as the most fragile creature of God's creation and I felt the need to take care of her. It was as if the roles had been reversed and now I needed to caress and take care of my big sister.

Chay wanted music at her celebration, so we made sure to invite some of the best artists of our time, artists that Chay admired and who admired Chay. Among them were Ana Gabriel, Joan Sebastian, Los Horóscopos, Larry Hernández, and Olga Tañón. Chay's manager, Pete Salgado, helped us plan the spectacular event and no detail was spared in making it the graduation of a Queen.

In addition to the musical performances, we organized it so that Chay's closest friends and immediate family members had a few minutes to speak. Everyone—my mom, my dad, my brothers, Chay's children, Pete Salgado, and Pepe Garza, her mentor—got up on the podium and spoke. The whole ceremony unfolded during several hours but to me it flew by. In the midst of all the pain I was feeling, it was a breath of fresh air to hear other people talk about my sister's beautiful life—and not her death, which was all the media had been talking about. It was like spending a little more time with her. I had never experienced the death of a loved one before and in that moment, I understood how important it is to have a ritual where everyone comes together to celebrate a life. The intensity of emotions in the amphitheater was palpable and I felt blessed to be surrounded by so many people loving and missing the person I loved most in the world. I don't know that I wasn't entirely able to process what was going on, but I remember the whole thing in flashes—flashes of pain, joy, and devastation, all at the same time. When I see the videos of the ceremony, I can hardly believe how every member of our family was able to get up on that podium to speak. I was in awe of Johnny, who spoke with the poise and elegance of a grown man, not a little boy distraught over the death of his mommy. Chiquis, with what had recently transpired with her mom, was nervous about what the public would say to her but her words were so beautiful and so full of love for her adoring mother that I am sure there wasn't a soul in the world who doubted her devotion. Jenicka and Jacqie spoke and each sang Chay a song with their beautiful voices. Mikey would have made his mama proud with his thoughtful and compassionate words. My mother, my father, and my brothers all spoke to Chay from their hearts and I'm sure she was smiling down on us as we took turns to give her our final farewell. Daddy and Lupe each sang her a song before a silent, weeping crowd. The people in the audience were just as distraught as we were and from high up on the stage where we were all seated, I saw how everyone who was present that day loved her from the bottom of their hearts. They were hurting just like we were hurting, and I prayed that they could find peace.

During most of the ceremony, I had my eyes fixed on the cocoon.

But I was also doing all I could not to look at it.

When my turn came to speak, I was so nervous. I hadn't prepared anything—with everything that was going on how could I have even thought about putting pen to paper? And throughout the ceremony Pastor Pete asked me several times whether I was sure I could do it.

"Yes, I can do this!" I mumbled back at him, knowing that I had absolutely no idea what I was going to say. I just hoped God would help me find the right words in my heart.

As I made my way up to the podium, I had to walk past Pete and I was worried that he was going to ask me again. But he didn't. He just said, "You can do this."

I started to speak and before I knew it, all these words were coming out of my mouth.

"Before you knew Jenni Rivera, I knew her as Chay, my only sister," I said as I took the microphone. "It is such a great blessing that God has given me the gift of being her only sister; her first living doll.

"I have feared this day since I was seven years old and my sister and I talked about it several times. I would say, 'Sister, I cannot live without you.'

"I thought that when this day came, I would not be able to bear the pain, and perhaps I couldn't if it were not for God, who lives in me. God's Word says in Romans 8:28, 'All things work together for good to those who love the Lord and are called for His purpose.'

"Jenni Rivera loves God; the Rivera family loves God. Jenni is made for the purpose of God—and also the Rivera family, which means that all things work for good.

"God gave me my sister for forty-three years, and those years worked for good, and now she is given to me for all eternity as a sister—and that works for good.

"Not one day of our lives would go by without her saying 'Sister, I love you,' and I'd reply 'I love you.' She would answer, 'I love you more.' We would say this back and forth until one of us surrendered. Now that she has graduated to Heaven with our Father God, I let her win. I can tell her that maybe she loved me more, but I can take the time to say that I'll miss her every day of my life.

"If you see me with a smile one day, it is because God still has me standing, and if you ever see me cry, it's because God is healing my heart.

"Jenni Rivera left a huge legacy and that is God's plan. His plan continues and will make Jenni live forever. The suffering we have today is huge but short-lived compared to an eternity we will have with her in Heaven.

"All things work together for good. If God made this day my sister's graduation, this day works for good."

Looking at the casket, I continued my speech and I said, "'Sister, how are you?' And she would have answered, 'Sister I'm good; and you?'

"And now I can tell her, "I know you're good. Sister, you are always the first in everything, even to meet Jesus. You are the first and I am happy for you. Enjoy Him, kiss Him, and kiss His beautiful face for me. I love you, Sister, every day. Today is Tuesday and tomorrow I'll see you in heaven.

"God bless you."

When I heard that girl whose biggest fear was to lose her sister open her mouth and speak so coherently while standing in front of her sister's cocoon, I asked myself, *Who is she?* I have no idea how I was able to speak with such clarity when inside, I was a complete mess. "All things work for good," I said, and I meant it. I had just lost my sister; I was living through the worst days of my life, yet I knew, from what I had lived through up until that moment, that God works for good. I didn't know how or when, but I felt deep in my soul that this tragedy was going to work for good. That everything that has happened in my past—the sexual abuse, the abortion, the violent and abusive first marriage, and so much more—had somehow prepared me for this pivotal moment. And I needed to be up to the challenge.

Near the conclusion of the ceremony, my brother Pete read from the Scriptures, and I had asked him in advance to share some final words and give people hope. As Pete spoke, God reminded me of the Apostle Peter, who was grieving after he had lost his friend, Jesus. But after the Upper Room experience on the Day of Pentecost, Peter walked out to a huge crowd in Jerusalem and, filled with the Spirit, gave a message and three thousand people were added to the church.

God told me, "Rosie, you can be like that."

So when my turn came, I began my closing remarks by saying, "Maybe today is very painful for you, as it is for us. Perhaps you are asking yourself, 'How can I get over this? When will the pain end?' Perhaps today you realize you need something different in your life."

Then I told the audience how I had found the answers I had looked for all my life—and that they could do exactly the same. God loved me. I said, "Jesus has my sister in His hands and I want every one of her fans who followed her here on Earth to follow her into Heaven."

I was honored to let the world know that Jenni was at rest—and that those witnessing the event in the arena, watching on television, or listening by radio could find the same peace. I asked those who needed the Lord, "Please raise your hand and I will pray for you." I prayed with my eyes closed as I usually do, and when I opened them I saw about three thousand hands in the air.

My eyes filled with tears of pain and tears of joy—to know that someone is receiving Jesus in his or her heart always brings joy to my heart, even if it's crushed.

Outside the arena, men, women, and children watching on large media screens fell to their knees with their hands lifted to God. Only eternity will reveal the impact this had on the estimated audience of not just two, but several million who were watching or listening that day. Later I would hear story after story of people who had connected or reconnected with God that day and amid my devastation, it brought me joy to know that I had contributed to making a difference in people's lives in a moment of so much pain. Just as I'd dreamed it, just as God and I had discussed, my plan was coming true. Chay and I were working for God, just not in the way I had expected. And even though I would have much preferred for things never to end this way, I know God does everything for a reason and I do not, for an instant, doubt His intentions.

At the conclusion of Chay's Celestial Graduation, one by one, each member of the family came forward and placed a white rose on her coffin—embracing and kissing the red casket. Then those in attendance formed a line to pay their respects. One by one, they came to see my sister. The procession continued on for hours.

Twelve days later we had a small, intimate gathering for my sister's burial. There were no cameras, no fans . . . just family. It was a beautiful ceremony, fit for a queen, with a red carpet and music, just as Chay would have wanted. At the moment when her cocoon was being lowered, I felt as if the ground was being pulled from under my feet and all the strength and determination I had been carrying around for the previous three weeks just crumbled to pieces. I couldn't bear to think of life without Chay and for an instant I wanted, with all my heart, to throw myself into the grave with her. Without her, life would never be good again and I didn't even want to try. But the thought of the children—my daughter, Chay's children, and the baby growing inside me—stopped me in my tracks and from that moment on, no matter how sad I have felt or how much I miss my sister, I have never looked back. I know my place is here now, and when the time comes, my sister and I will be reunited in Heaven.

seventeen

healing

After we took Chay to her final resting place—Mama's Garden, as the kids chose to call it—on December 31, 2012, Abel, Kassey, and I moved into Chay's house in Encino. If I was going to act as her trustee, and the guardian of her children, I felt that I needed to be by their side at all times and when they needed me most. Chiquis also moved back into the house and in those first months, we all struggled to find our bearings. That big, beautiful house—my sister's dream house—was full of people, yet without her it felt so painfully empty.

I took on the leadership of Jenni Rivera Enterprises (JRE) and from the moment I stepped into my new role, I gave it my all. My sister always went above and beyond for me, so I was going to make sure I did the same. And to me that meant giving a hundred and ten percent—sometimes to a fault. I was still pregnant at the time yet I worked day and night, doing my best to handle things and keep her empire running, always hoping that I was making the right decisions and that she would have approved.

It was a difficult time. There have been so many difficult times in my life, but 2013 was by far the hardest year I've ever had to live. Not only did I lose my sister; I lost my life. Practically overnight I went from being the Riveras' anonymous little sister, working her nine-to-five job and preaching on the weekends, to being Jenni Rivera's trustee, the keeper of her legacy. I had trouble finding myself in this new paradigm where I was constantly being watched and never had a minute to myself. I missed my anonymity and just being able to go get ice cream with my family or go for a run in the park. But my biggest challenge, and what I simply couldn't understand, was how I was supposed to continue living without my sister in the world. In the days and weeks after her burial, I walked around like a zombie. That old familiar feeling of not wanting to live any longer came back to haunt me and I found myself torn between my duties to my sister and the internal turmoil that was taking over my mind and my heart. All the emotions I had been able to somewhat keep at bay while we were planning the Celestial Graduation and the burial came flooding out and I wasn't always able to control them. If I had been left to my own devices, I would have probably holed up and cried for days and days but I had to keep it together and fulfill my promise to my sister.

It was so hard. At the Gibson I had said to the world, "All things work for good," and I knew in my heart that God had taken my sister for a reason, but I was not yet able to see what that reason was. "Why didn't you take me with her, God?" I'd ask Him. I was the one who had always wanted to die; I was the one who had begged Him, for years and years, to end my life. Chay wanted to live. She *always* wanted to live. She was going to be eighty and still rocking the world, touching hearts and swaying souls. There was no one more alive than Chay; she had dreams and plans—her whole life was about the present and the future, whereas for as long as I could remember, I had wanted to die. Granted, with Abel by my side and God in my heart, I was in a much better place than before, but I still knew that being in Heaven is better than being in this cruel world. And knowing that made me want to die even more, because I wanted to be close to God. How could He allow this to happen? Yet I knew there was a reason. There *had* to be a reason. I just wasn't seeing it yet. The pain was blinding me.

Grieving the death of a loved one is something everyone does in his or her own way, and it is something that all of us, in one way or another, will have to do. There is no right or wrong way to do it; there is just the way that is right for you. Some people need a lot of time, others just a few days, or weeks. Some need to talk about it with everyone around them, while others prefer to keep it private.

In my case, the process has happened very slowly. I have had many conversations with God, trying to understand why she had to go so soon. In one of my attempts to deal with my pain, I went to see a Christian grief counselor. I went through counseling the same way I saw many therapists after my sexual abuse. I guess that after so many years of keeping terrible secrets to myself, I finally learned the value of talking and analyzing what goes through my mind and heart. In my sessions, I talked about the pain I was feeling, how angry I was at God for having taken her away from me, how heartbroken I was to have to live without her. The counselor heard me out, made a few points, and then he suddenly said something that shifted my entire world. Instead of delving deeper into my feelings of loss and disappointment, he just asked me to pray with him. He put his hands together and said:

"Thank you, God, for Jenni."

At that moment it dawned on me: all this time I had been so upset at God for taking her away from me that I had forgotten to thank Him for the thirty-one years I had her. And I had to thank Him because He didn't just give me a sister (we all know that there are good sisters, and there are not-so-good sisters). He gave me The Most Amazing Sister in the World. She wasn't only an unbelievable performer, an inspiring woman, an extraordinary mother. She was the most incredible sister: the person who never let me down, who never talked down to me or scolded me, and when I was wrong, she'd tell me but always with such love that I never felt ashamed. She knew of all my mistakes and all my flaws and even so, she still loved me. She was the one person in the world who always, always, stood by my side. So many people go through life without experiencing even a fraction of that, and I had had it for thirty-one years. That's when I started to find some peace; my sister was a light that shone so bright that if God had to take her, it was okay because for the time I had her, it was amazing.

The truth is, I don't think I'll ever get over losing my sister without God. As time goes by, I've learned to deal with it better because God has begun to heal my heart but it's still a process to complete healing. She was the most important person in my life. And no matter how much comfort I may find in my family and in God, not a day goes by when I don't wish I could hug her just one more time. But I know I will, on a Wednesday in Heaven.

My sister left me in charge of her businesses and her legacy, but of all the responsibilities she left me with, the one that mattered most was taking care of her children. I saw my sister break her back to provide for her kids, whether it was back in the days when she was selling real estate in Long Beach, or later when she became a recording artist. Her schedule was always jam-packed with things to do—she traveled from gigs to press conferences to charity events to TV appearances and even though what she loved most in the world was to be home and spend time with her kids, every day she would wake up and hit the road to build a better life for them, the best life possible. Chiquis, Jacqie, Mikey, Jenicka, and Johnny are five extraordinary human beings. They each carry a little part of Chay; it comforts me to know that she continues to live through each and every one of them.

Chay always said that being a mom was her favorite job and she was great at it. And with her no longer here to look after them, I made them my number one priority. Everything that had to do with *my* dreams and *my* life was put on hold. It wasn't a sacrifice; it wasn't an effort—it's what I wanted to do. In 2012, I had started working on this book and recording an album but none of that was going to happen because my sister needed me. My nieces' and nephews' comfort, their well-being, became more important to me than my own. I even asked my husband to put his dreams on hold—Abel is an incredible singer and he was working to record his first album, but the minute my life changed, he dropped everything to support me. He took care of the house, the kids, everything that needed to run smoothly so I could do my new job in the best way possible.

When it came to taking care of the kids, things weren't as simple as they might seem. Johnny and Jenicka had just lost their mother, they had recently lost their father, and their little hearts had so much healing to do. But as much as I wanted to help them every step of the way, one of the things I had to learn was to give them love and care without being overbearing and controlling. I needed to make sure they could continue with their lives the way they wanted them to be. In fact, I went to counseling to learn how to help them grieve and the child psychologist I met with advised me that life had to remain as close to normal as possible. I needed to make sure they didn't have to confront too many changes considering how much had already changed with the fact that their mother wasn't there anymore. I had to navigate a fine line between giving them the space they needed to grieve while giving Chiquis her place as their true guardian, and I had to keep being their loving aunt, making sure they knew in their hearts that they aren't orphans because they will always have us, their family. Sometimes they resisted my presence and while I totally understood and responded by giving them more space and privacy, I worried all the time that I was letting my sister down by not taking proper care of her babies.

Six months after Chay's accident, on July 24, 2013, Abel and I welcomed our beautiful baby girl into the world. A true Rivera, she didn't make her entrance like a normal baby in a hospital bed but in a car!

I was in Chay's office when my water broke and no one else was in the house. She and I were alone. Ever since her departure, Chay is always with me so I knew I didn't have to be afraid because she was going to help me through it.

Abel had gone out to get us lunch and because I had been in labor for thirty-five hours with Kassey, I didn't even bother to call him, I was so convinced we had time. I finished up what I was doing and about thirty minutes later I texted him "Babe my water broke. No worries, we have time." Abel of course arrived immediately, all hurried and nervous only to find me casually shaving my legs in the shower. Because I was so calm, he started recording me and I was joking and being cute for the camera—saying I was doing so well I could pop out two babies if I wanted to—when suddenly, within ten minutes, my contractions went from perfectly tolerable to absolutely insane. As soon as the contractions gave me a breather, I jumped out of the shower and managed to put on a bra and a skirt—thank God for the skirt because it ended up being the perfect escape route for the baby! Abel rushed after me with a shirt and the diaper bag.

Within a matter of minutes, we were in the car on the way to the hospital. I was in excruciating pain. I hiked my feet up on the dashboard and before I knew it, the baby's head popped out! We were completely panicked, and in my pain-induced stupor I didn't know whether I should push or try to hold the baby in until we got to the hospital. Abel pulled up on the side of the road and got on the phone with 911, who told him what he needed to do to deliver the baby. There, on the corner of Havenhurst and Esprit at one thirty p.m., our youngest daughter was born. Following instructions from 911, Abel tied the umbilical cord with his shoelace so our baby girl could take her first breath in this world.

We named her Samantha Chay. My sister loved giving everyone nicknames and "Samalia," "Sam," or "Sammy" is what she called me when I was growing up. "Chay" is the nickname Juan and I gave to her, so in Sammy Chay, my sister and I are united once again. I named my daughter after Chay, the amazing woman I knew and I pray she inherits my sister's extraordinary characteristics of love, mercy, work ethic, generosity and passion. And I'd love Sammy Chay to have my sister's personality from being a morning person to giving it all for things she believed in. The birth was on a Wednesday—Chay's favorite day of the week. In sharing the good news via Twitter, I wrote, "Yesterday was Tuesday and today I saw my sister. Thank You, God, because today, on a Wednesday, Chay helped pass a beautiful baby girl from Your arms into my arms."

That first year we all worked around the clock to make Chay's legacy shine, but as weeks turned into months, and months turned into years, I started to see how the intensity of my dedication was taking a toll on my family. JRE took over my existence and I would take care of more of my duties there than I'd take care of myself and my pregnancy. I wouldn't sleep, I'd barely eat—all I cared about was JRE and the children. If Jenicka needed to talk or Johnny needed help with his homework, I wanted to be there. Not because they asked that of me, but because I felt it was my duty. If there was anything I could do to make their lives better, that became my priority.

"Go get some rest, *Tía*. Don't worry we can talk tomorrow," the kids would say to me sometimes. "*Tía*, go be with your family. We're okay."

I worried about them so much and even though I knew that it wasn't in my hands to offer them solace, I never wanted them to feel lonely or lost. I was so preoccupied with them that year that God knows I didn't give my sweet Kassey all the attention she deserved. Deep in my mind, I thought, *Even if I'm not present, at least my daughter has her mother—Chay's kids don't even have that. They need me more, right now. Kassey and I will have time later.* But time is a tricky thing. You always think you'll have more of it, until one day you don't. And if Chay's death had taught me anything, it was that.

Abel perfectly understood everything that was going through

my mind, but he started to worry about what this frenzy was doing to our family.

"You know, wife, JRE isn't more important than our family," he'd say to me. "What about our daughter? And our baby? You need to take care of them too."

When Abel started to say these things I realized that I was going too far. That wasn't what my sister would have wanted. Yes, she wanted me to help preserve her legacy for the sake of the kids; she wanted me to take care of JRE, but she would have never wanted me to put that before my husband and my daughters. She knew how much I had struggled to find true love and now that I had a man who didn't just love me, but also loved my big crazy family, she wouldn't have wanted me to let that go. So I began to take a step back and while I was still there to support the kids in anything they needed, I was able to make time to take care of my family as well.

Abel, Kassey, Sammy, and I lived in Chay's house until the fall of 2014. The year and a half that we spent there with Chiquis and the kids was overwhelming and difficult, but also beautiful and incredibly special. Yet Chay's house is their house and it was time for us to move on. Had it not been for their love and support along with that of the rest of my family, I'm not sure I would have been able to make it through the many challenges I had to face those first years. Their strength inspired me to be strong and on so many occasions, it felt as though they were taking care of me.

It wasn't an easy decision to make—especially since Kassey had become so attached to her cousins and she didn't want to leave—but it was the right decision for my family. My husband needed to have his own house, his own space, and so did I. Now that Sammy was getting bigger, it became important that we find a place of our own.

Then there was also the question of the guardianship.

While there was indeed a signed document that said I was Jenicka and Johnny's legal guardian, I had decided that December ninth that Chiquis should be the one to take care of them and handle the day-to-day. She is the person who knows them best, the person who has always taken care of them whenever Chay was working or on the road. Yet a few situations occurred when it was unfair that Chiquis should have to go through me to do what she knows best. One day, for example, she wanted to take the kids on a trip but when she went to get passports for them, she couldn't do so without my signature. It happened a few other times, enough for Chiquis and me to decide that it was time to make the switch. We had already discussed it in December 2012, but these situations confirmed that the time was right. I love my niece and nephew so much but never, while I was living with them, did I expect or even try to replace their mama. I always wanted it to be very clear that I am their aunt and while I love them and support them with all my heart, I can never replace their mother.

Giving up the guardianship, although it was the right thing to do, was so hard. I felt as if I was betraying my sister's trust, as if I was betraying her final will. When someone dies, you have the tendency to want to leave everything exactly the way they wanted—the bed, the room, the shower, everything. You want to preserve that person's presence in this world as much as possible, and although I knew in my heart that it was the right thing to do, I didn't want her to ever feel as though I had let her down, or shied away from my responsibilities. I wanted to make sure that when I get to Heaven and see my sister again, I'll be able to tell her, "Sister,

I took good care of your kids, your beautiful, precious kids." And in this case, taking care of her kids meant giving Chiquis what was already hers—what has always been hers. The only thing that mattered at this point was what Chiquis, Jenicka, and Johnny needed most. Chiquis, in particular, lost her mom long before the rest of us did and on top of that she lost her home, her siblings, her privacy, and her dignity. I took all of Chiquis's losses and I tried to carry them, and that was when I decided to give the guardianship back to her because I knew it meant more to Chiquis than all the money in the world. I wish I could give her back everything she had lost, but at least *this* I can do. And we are all better off because of it.

As I continue to take each day as it comes, I can say that yes, "all things work for good." If I knew it in my mind at the time of Chay's passing, I now know it in my heart. Losing my sister has been the hardest experience I've ever had to live through but thanks to it, I am stronger than I've ever been. Losing my sister was my biggest fear, the one thing I thought I would never be able to survive, but here I am, and I have survived. I didn't throw myself in the casket. I didn't lose my mind or become depressed, all thanks to God and my family.

I'm not here to prove anything to anyone; my only intention is to share my story with the hope of inspiring others in their time of need. I spent my entire life wanting people to like me—whether it was my family, in front of a camera, or with the men I dated—all I cared about was pleasing others, feeling loved. But when I figured out that God loved me regardless of who I was or what I did in my past, I felt so free! His love is so great that it instantly moved me to stop drinking and smoking, having sex, because I no longer needed any of that. God's love was so great that I could just feed off of that love.

Every single thing that happened in my life prepared me for what was to come. Being my sister's trustee inherently comes with a lot of power and authority, but because I have been abused—and because sexual abuse is an abuse of power—I'm probably more careful than what I might have been if I hadn't gone through everything I've endured. And of course my sister knew that.

So today, I can thank God for the humility and wisdom I gained from my broken past—the eighteen years of crying and suffering, the abusive relationships, the sexual abuse. Those eighteen years softened up a heart that could have been prideful, that could have been greedy or angry, because with what life had offered me, everything on a silver platter, I could have been the most horrible, self-centered, and greedy human being ever to walk the earth. But all those years of suffering, all that pain, made me humble, and now I can handle the pain as well as everything the world has to offer. I can be on a reality show, with all those people hating me and loving me and then hating me again, but it doesn't matter to me because what other people think no longer has the power to change who I am. Only I do. And I'm proud of who I am. When I look back at the wild ride my life has been, I am proud of how far I have come and the person I've become. Despite everything I have been through, I am at a place where I am finally living the life I was intended to live—a life full of love and happiness and where everything is possible.

Everything works for good. My sister is resting now and I believe she didn't feel the pain of the accident. We are all in pain, but she is up in Heaven with our Lord Jesus Christ and she can look down on us and see that even though it still hurts, we are all doing well. Jenicka just graduated high school early, with honors, and is attending college and turning her amazing photography into art for merchandise. Johnny is going to graduate two years early and is designing shirts and his mother's newest perfume. Chiquis is flourishing in her new career and she has gotten back a little bit of what she lost through the love of her fans. My children are doing much better, they have their mama back, and now that things have calmed down a bit, Abel has started to record a few songs. Jacqie and I continue to be very close friends and I named her president of the Jenni Rivera Love Foundation, where she excels by donating time and funds to the battered women's shelter, called A Butterfly's Beginning, in Long Beach. Juan and I continue to work together on preserving Chay's legacy, including her albums, concerts, videos, books, as well as the fund-raising concert JenniVive. My mother goes to Mama's Garden four times a week to make sure her Janney has fresh flowers, and my father continues to produce some of her music and writes songs for her. Mikey is working on the Paloma Project, making murals of his mother all over the nation. He has three to date and the most beautiful one is at the Jenni Rivera Memorial Park in Long Beach. He also works at the online store . . . With love and humility he fulfills each order himself. He is a wonderful father; he learned it from his mama. Gus works on the Jenni Rivera La Gran Señora Tequila and behind the scenes he dedicates endless hours to making JenniVive happen. At his church, Pastor Pete has received hundreds of Jenni Rivera fans who are hurting after Jenni's death and he leads them to healing and salvation through Christ.

Lupe continues with his career and although he has distanced himself from the family, I am one hundred percent certain that we will be reunited—not necessarily because of us, but because I have faith in God and His plan for this family. There is a bigger plan for all this and we need to hang in there despite the fact that we miss him so deeply. Although Lupe asked me for space, and I am giving it to him, one day I hope to make the journey to his home to take responsibility for my actions, in the hopes of mending our broken relationship. It has been very difficult to live this new phase of my life without him and although I need my brother, I respect his wishes because I love him so much.

In April 2015, Abel, Kassey, Sammy, and I moved into a beautiful new house and we are relishing the time we have to be together, just to be ourselves. This is the first time we are in a house that isn't Chay's or my mother's since 2012, and here I have finally started to feel like Rosie again. I'm still in charge of my sister's company and I still focus all my energy on making her legacy grow, but for the first time in a long time, I'm starting to allow myself to dream again. I've allowed myself to be that little girl again, sitting on her father's lap, dreaming of conquering the world.

I don't know yet what my next dream will be, but I'm excited for what the future holds. Every day is a new adventure and while there are moments when sadness and pain still overwhelm my soul, I know that God loves me and with Him by my side, all things work for good. My heart was broken, but I offered the pieces to Jesus and because of Him, I have been made whole. I can trip, I can fall, but I will always get back on my feet because God is in my heart. I can tell my abuser what I planned for eighteen years: "You couldn't break me." And as long as God walks with me, nothing can.

acknowledgments

Writing a book is a team effort, and this one was no exception.

To everyone at Penguin Random House and Celebra—Raymond, Kim, Kio and Andrea—for being a wonderful team that made this dream a reality.

To Marissa Matteo, for introducing me to Raymond Garcia, and making the initial and ultimately divine connection happen.

To Neil Eskelin for helping me write this book and believing in my story and its potential when no one even knew my name.

To my local church for their constant support in helping me find myself.

To my family for loving me in spite of my bad attitude and strong character and especially for believing me about the sexual abuse the moment I told them.

To my children for allowing Mommy to love and focus on achieving her dreams.

To my husband, the gentle, patient, merciful man who never asks me about my past and loves me enough to let me shine brightly.

acknowledgments

To every single abused woman who has told me her story and cried in my arms, you gave me the passion and purpose to speak up—love can't remain silent.

To Christ for making me whole and giving me my voice.

Thank you.